The Language of Success

The Language of Success

*Business Writing That Informs,
Persuades, and Gets Results*

TOM SANT

American Management Association

New York * Atlanta * Brussels * Chicago * Mexico City * San Francisco
Shanghai * Tokyo * Toronto * Washington, D.C.

Special discounts on bulk quantities of AMACOM books are
available to corporations, professional associations, and other
organizations. For details, contact Special Sales Department,
AMACOM, a division of American Management Association,
1601 Broadway, New York, NY 10019.
Tel: 212-903-8316. Fax: 212-903-8083.
E-mail: specialsls@amanet.org
Website: www.amacombooks.org/go/specialsales
To view all AMACOM titles go to: www.amacombooks.org

This publication is designed to provide accurate and authoritative information
in regard to the subject matter covered. It is sold with the understanding that
the publisher is not engaged in rendering legal, accounting, or other
professional service. If legal advice or other expert assistance is required, the
services of a competent professional person should be sought.

Library of Congress Cataloging-in-Publication Data

Sant, Tom.
   The language of success : business writing that informs, persuades, and gets results /
Tom Sant.
      p. cm.
   Includes index.
   ISBN 978-0-8144-7473-0 (pbk.)
1. Business writing.   2. Business communication.   I. Title.
   HF5718.3.S26 2008
   658.4′53—dc22

2007038999

Printing number

10 9 8 7 6 5 4 3 2 1

To Susan
You have a natural gift for
communicating kindness and love.

Contents

Chapter 3   The Principles: Modern Methods in Business Writing   55

Chapter 4   The Practice: Real-World Applications of the Language of Success   127

Acknowledgments

Writing is a fundamental part of my life and has been as long as I can remember. I owe a debt of gratitude to some excellent English teachers along the way who awakened in me an appreciation for clear writing. I was lucky in high school to have two teachers in particular who were tough but inspiring: Percy Totheroh and Joyce King. Mrs. King, who had been a magazine editor and who put in hours correcting and editing everything we wrote, taught me more about effective writing than anyone or anything else.

This book has benefited from careful readings and thoughtful editing by a number of people. In particular, I want to acknowledge the excellent help my son, Chris Sant, gave me. Editing somebody else's writing is a thankless task, but he took the job on with good grace and perceptive insight. He pointed out as gently as possible each time I violated my own principles. Thanks, Chris! The other person who was particularly helpful is my wife and partner, Susan Hirsch. Because she has a thoroughly pragmatic point of view, acquired during her career as a successful business leader, she consistently has kept me focused on delivering a message that other business people will value. Thanks, Susan!

Finally, for all the help I received from others, any deficiencies in the book are solely my responsibility.

The Language of Success

CHAPTER 1

Introduction

Where We're Going and Why the Trip Is Worth Taking

This book is about words, about the damage that can be done when they are used ineffectively, and about the power to be gained when they are used well. The purpose of this book is to show you how to write more effectively. It's designed to help you produce the kinds of documents that are likely to be part of your professional life—documents that ask and answer questions, that provide information other people need to do their jobs, that communicate your opinions, or that persuade, instruct, or update. We'll emphasize e-mail as the primary medium for delivering most of these messages for several reasons. First, e-mail has obviously become the dominant mode of communication all over the world. Second, it's different enough from traditional ink-on-paper writing that it poses its own unique set of challenges. Along the way, I'll provide examples of both good and bad writing for you to consider, explaining what works and what doesn't so that you can adapt the ideas quickly to your own use.

So that's where we're going. Admittedly, writing is a skill that most people embrace reluctantly at best. But it's a skill that can make a huge difference in your career. From a practical standpoint, few professional accomplishments will pay off more in terms of your personal success or the success of your company or organization than learning to communicate effectively.

In my experience, most people don't like to write. There are exceptions, of course. I'm one of them. I usually enjoy writing, especially if there's room for creativity or if there's a challenge to the task. Lots of people make their living as writers, in fields like technical writing, marketing communications, journalism, public relations, sales support, proposal writing, speech writing, and so on. You have to figure most of them don't mind writing. Other professions are virtually inseparable from the need to write—higher education, for example, where you must "publish or perish," or the practice of law, where letters, contracts, and other documents are often the deliverable for which the client is paying. All the same, the people who love to write are clearly in the minority. For the vast majority of people in the workforce, writing is a necessary evil. It's something they have to do, but they don't see it as a core part of their professional responsibility. Writing isn't part of their "real" job, they'll tell you.

But, of course, they are wrong.

Over the past fifteen or twenty years, the nature of work has changed dramatically. More valuable than any other raw material or resource, knowledge has become the engine of economic growth and the primary driver of increased productivity. The fact is we have now completed the shift to a knowledge-based workforce, a shift just as significant in its own right as was the shift to an industrial workforce in the late nineteenth century. During the past ten years, for the first time in world history, over half of the gross domestic product of the major Western economies has been directly linked to knowledge-based activities. As a result, businesses, institutions of higher learning, government agencies, and others in this knowledge-based economy now place greater importance than ever before on finding, sharing, and using information as efficiently as possible. Useful, valuable knowledge has become the fundamental source of differentiation for both organizations and individuals.

The concept of useful and valuable knowledge is worth examining. It means doing more than simply sharing information. Facts, details, instructions, and other forms of data may be necessary, but they tend to have less value than *informed insight*. Think about the money and effort that organizations put into identifying and implementing "best practices." Owners and senior managers don't want some checklist of steps to follow when performing a certain task or a template for organizing certain processes. What they want is deeper insight into business process, insight that will enable them to improve bottom line results. In a knowledge-based economy, progress is measured by such factors as increased innovation, improved productivity, or better financial performance. As a result, implementing best practices is not merely a matter of collecting facts and data, but rather of identifying and disseminating knowledge. And that requires clear, effective, flexible communication.

In a knowledge-based economy, our success and our organization's progress depend on our ability to communicate with our bosses, our subordinates, our colleagues and our customers.

Sometimes people need us to provide factual details and other forms of explicit information that are relatively uncomplicated. *Here is the company's current mileage allowance on expense accounts. How to change your password. The new starting time for the budget review meeting. Some unexpected results from our recent lab tests of titanium alloys. Third quarter sales results showed a 2 percent decline in our core markets.* In

Words to Write By . . .

Success in today's knowledge-based economy is based on the ability to write effectively.

these situations, we are providing others with the information they need to do their jobs. This is an important task and early in our career it's likely to be the kind of writing we do most often.

As we advance, as we acquire more experience and responsibility, people are likely to turn to us to provide deeper insights into the *why* behind those facts. *Why should I change my password? What do you think caused those unexpected results you got from the new titanium alloys? Why did our sales go down in the third quarter?* What they want from us now is our opinion, presumably based on our training and experience. By providing facts in combination with our expert opinion about what those facts mean, we have taken on a more complex communication challenge. As we move up in our organization, particularly if we achieve recognition as a technical expert or if we have a management role, we will do a lot more of this kind of writing.

Sometimes we need to write messages that the audience isn't looking for at all. In these instances, we write because we need to motivate employees; we need to persuade customers, convince management, or possibly assure investors. *Let's prevent any further data losses by adhering to our information security standards! Three reasons we should change the design specs of our engine housing. The long-term outlook for the housing downturn and our plan to stabilize earnings.* In these situations, we may provide facts and offer some opinions, but what matters ultimately is our ability to affect what our readers think, what they feel, or how they act. As you rise higher in an organization, you will find yourself doing a lot more motivating and inspiring than simple information sharing. This is a much more difficult task than simply providing information or even offering an opinion, but it's usually a much more important one, too.

In the next section are two examples of e-mails written and sent out by the heads of major corporations. Both messages are grammatically "correct." Both are pretty clear. Both were apparently intended to motivate the recipients. But by any reasonable standard, both messages failed to communicate. In fact, they failed so badly that they created major problems for the men who wrote them and the companies they led.

Igniting Firestorms

On September 11, 2001, life as we knew it stood still for a moment. The heartbeat of society paused. You probably remember exactly where you were and what you were doing as you watched the twin towers crumble to earth, as you saw a corner of the mighty Pentagon burning.

Millions of people went into shock. Frantically, we wondered: Is it possible someone I know, someone I love, might have been on one of those deadly flights? Who do I know who lives or works in New York? In Washington? Were they safe? No one knew much. Facts were scarce. People huddled together at work and in public spaces, clustering around televisions that endlessly repeated videotape loops of the horror. We drew our family closer to us that night. For days, maybe weeks afterward, we felt emotionally bruised. We tried to be kinder to each other, a little more patient. It was a difficult time, but in our shared grief and fear we sought to comfort one another.

Perhaps that helps explain the reaction of the employees of one large business concern based in the United States when they received a message from the founder and CEO of their company late in the evening on 9/11. Would he have a kind word, they wondered? Perhaps a moment of shared reflection or a personal connection?

When they clicked on the e-mail he had sent them, this is the message they got from their leader, a man we will call "Bob":

From: Bob Teufel
Sent: Tuesday, September 11, 2001 9:45 PM
To: The Entire Teufel Team
Subject: Staying Focused

Today we all experienced a tragedy that we will never forget. It will leave its mark on us and on the United States for generations to come.

However, we must not allow this tragedy to distract us from our purpose.

We have polled our offices and learned that we suffered no losses to members of the Teufel Team. Our facilities are open for business. So let's stay focused and get back to work!

We have a warehouse full of products that must ship. We have new designs that must be approved. We have revenue targets we need to beat. Our customers expect us to give our promises to them. We need to support one another by keeping our attention focused on the job at hand.

We are open for business in the United States and in 22 countries around the world. I am confident each of you will refocus your energy and show up tomorrow morning, ready to get the job done!

Thanks.

Bob

Imagine how comforting that message was! About as comforting as pouring rubbing alcohol on an open wound. "Okay, everybody, snap out of it and get back to work! We have a new product that needs to ship on time. Stop your sniveling and get back to what really matters—making money!"

Maybe this e-mail was just an expression of frustration from an executive who saw one more obstacle thrown in his path as he barreled toward status as one of the mega-wealthy. Whatever it was supposed to be, it failed.

A friend of mine worked at this company in September 2001. His immediate reaction to the e-mail was that it was the most insensitive, self-serving, incompetent piece of writing he had seen in thirty years of business experience. From the moment that e-mail arrived, his primary goal was to escape from the business enterprise where he had worked for several years. All he wanted was to find a job somewhere else, a place where the leadership could at least pretend to feel normal human emotions. He left a few months later.

Apparently he wasn't alone in his reaction. He told me that he didn't meet a single person among all his fellow employees who could get past the utter insensitivity of the message. In fact, it provoked a tidal wave of anger and disgust among employees. Morale plummeted. *What kind of person is he?* they wondered. This is a boss who doesn't care about us as people, they concluded, and he doesn't seem to care about anything that doesn't have a financial value. Not about the thousands of dead and injured, not about our personal security, not even about the fate of the nation. All he cares about is meeting the quarterly numbers to keep the stock price up.

The reaction got ugly very fast, so in an effort toward damage control, the vice president of HR issued a two-page e-mail the next day, taking a completely different tone. He announced that the company would set up a fund for the victims of 9/11 with the company matching all employee donations.

A nice gesture, but it came too late. The mask had slipped. Thanks to a thoughtless message, the CEO's credibility was shot, and employee loyalty was seriously damaged. In spite of all the gestures, my friend's own opinion of the e-mail hasn't changed to this day. He still gets angry just talking about it.

The point of this story is not that a particular business leader demonstrated appalling judgment and displayed a spiritual emptiness of Saharan proportions. Rather, the point is that a single thoughtless message, tossed out upon the e-mail grid, can wreak instant havoc that is virtually impossible to fix. What we write and how we write it matters as never before. Writing well has always mattered in business, of course. What's different now is the unparalleled power and reach of e-mail. Our mistakes are no longer confined to a small group of people who may not have had the highest of expectations for us. Now they are broadcast for the whole world to see.

Screaming in Print

The impact can be devastating. As *The Wall Street Journal,* the *Daily Telegraph of London,* and other leading publications reported in April 2001, Cerner Corporation's stock price dropped over 20 percent after a blistering e-mail written by the CEO, attacking his senior management team for laziness and incompetence, was leaked to the press. The CEO, Neal Patterson, threatened to fire managers who didn't shape up and gave them two weeks to whip their employees into shape. His e-mail, which had the subject line "MANAGEMENT DIRECTIVE: Fix it or changes will be made," was sent to all headquarters managers with "high importance."

> We are getting less than 40 hours of work from a large number of our KC-based EMPLOYEES. The parking lot is sparsely used at 8AM; likewise at 5PM. As managers—you either do not know what your EMPLOYEES are doing; or you do not CARE. . . .
>
> NEVER in my career have I allowed a team which worked for me to think they had a 40 hour job. I have allowed YOU to create a culture which is permitting this. NO LONGER.

The e-mail then goes on to list six punitive steps that the CEO is taking, effective immediately (or, effective IMMEDIATELY, as he no doubt would have put it). These enlightened steps include closing the employee center, implementing a time clock system and requiring all employees to punch in and out, freezing all promotions, cutting staff by 5 percent across the board, and so on. Just so his managers understood where they stood in this little Greek tragedy playing out on the windswept prairies of Kansas, he told them, "If you are [part of] the problem, pack your bags."

He went on to say that he knows "the parking lot is not a great measurement for 'effort'" and that results are ultimately what counts. But he doesn't care. "I am through with the debate," he told them. "My measurement will be the parking lot: It should be substantially full at 7:30 AM and 6:30 PM." He orders his management team to call some 7 AM and 6 PM and Saturday morning meetings immediately. It doesn't matter whether there's anything to meet about, apparently. "The pizza man should show up at 7:30 PM to feed the starving teams working late," he writes.

Folks this is a management problem, not an EMPLOYEE problem. Congratulations, you are management. You have the responsibility for our EMPLOYEES. I will hold you accountable. You have allowed this to get to this state. You have two weeks. Tick, tock.

Gosh, I can't imagine why Wall Street reacted so badly to this little love letter when someone posted it anonymously on a Yahoo financial message board, can you? Aside from the aberrant use of capitals to let his managers understand he is SO SERIOUS ABOUT THIS THAT HE HAS TO SCREAM AT THEM, of course. And aside from the manic tone. Oh, and aside from the sheer illogic of demanding that people show up early and hang around late, regardless of what the financial performance of the company suggests. (The company was doing very well at that point, thank you.)

No, perhaps it was simply the core message: Something very bad has apparently happened at this company, the management team is viewed by the CEO as being lazy and/or incompetent, and the person at the top appears to be a little unstable. Stephen Davas of Goldman Sachs was quoted by the *Daily Telegraph* as saying, rather tactfully, I think, that this e-mail "raised two real questions for investors. Has anything changed at Cerner to cause such a seemingly violent reaction? And is this a chief executive that investors are comfortable with?" Whatever the cause, investors began selling the stock as fast as they could, and Cerner's share price dropped 22 percent in just three days.

After the sound of his stock tumbling into the basement got his attention, Patterson, the author of the e-mail, undid the caps lock on his computer and apologized to his entire staff. It's all a big misunderstanding, he said. No harm intended. He claimed that he was just trying to motivate his managers. "I did it with a lot of satire, never thinking it would be communicated to my associates or broadcast to the outside," he explained. "But I lit the match. That match has started a firestorm."[1]

Well, Neal, I guess it just goes to show that not everybody has the gift for satire. That "tick, tock" thing at the end was pretty clever. Creepy, but clever.

Ah, the beauties of technology. The fact that both of these gaffes were broadcast over e-mail meant they were able to offend many more people much faster. Thanks to the World Wide Web, when we do something boneheaded nowadays, people in Sri Lanka and Uruguay and Wall Street can read it or watch it the next day. And dump our stock as a result.

Just to be clear, I'm not saying e-mail caused the problems with these two "motivational" messages. The CEOs who wrote them caused the problems. They created insensitive, rude, ineffective messages. It's just that e-mail made the bad consequences happen faster and more widely once their messages were sent. And e-mail can do the same for you. Oh, joy.

Living in the Midst of Revolution

As I write this, I'm sitting on a train traveling north from London toward Manchester. All around me, other travelers are passing the time in the usual ways—reading novels, skimming through newspapers, dozing, chatting, eating, and working. None of these activities are much different from what a rail traveler might have done in 1860 or even in 1990.

But there is one activity going on around me that a visitor from years past would find incomprehensible. Everywhere I look, people are working on their e-mail.

Some of them are sending and receiving e-mail over their laptop computers, using a wireless connection to the Internet available to

[1]Source: *Fortune*, "Oops," Monday April 16, 2001.

passengers on the train. Others are using cellular connections into a telecommunications carrier to receive and send e-mails from their Blackberries or other handheld devices.

Just before I started typing this, I was among them. While hurtling through the darkness somewhere between London and Manchester, I read and answered an e-mail from my 85-year-old mother who had a question about selling her house. I dealt with another from my business partner, asking if I was available to do three days of consulting in Istanbul at the end of May. And I dealt with a dozen or more other messages from clients, prospects, friends, and other members of my family.

For most of you, the response to all this is probably "ho-hum, what's new?" At most you might have thought, "You can do e-mail on the train in England? Cool!" Otherwise, none of this sounds all that unusual.

But it's actually quite remarkable. Unless you are a teenager, you can remember when such wireless connectivity was impossible. And if you are 35 or older, you remember when there was no such thing as e-mail. Now, Internet access and the use of e-mail as a primary means of communication are virtually universal, ranging from octogenarians like my mother to young children barely able to identify the letters on a keyboard.

The explosive growth of e-mail is mind-boggling, especially considering that Ray Tomlinson sent the first e-mail message in 1982. And what did that first message say? Was it something like, "What hath God wrought" or "Dr. Watson, come here, I need you," or perhaps "One small step for e-mail, one giant inbox for mankind"? No, as far as Tomlinson can remember, it was a message telling everybody else in his work group to use the @ sign to designate the recipient's host computer when sending a message. In other words, the first e-mail message simply announced its own existence. (Rumor has it that Tomlinson received three spam messages approximately fifteen minutes later, including a very attractive financial proposition from the widow of former Foreign Minister Chester Mongaweba of Nigeria.)

E-Mail is the true "killer app" that has made the Internet indispensable. In fact, e-mail has grown so rapidly it now exceeds all other forms of written communication for business and personal use

by several orders of magnitude. In 2006, according to some estimates, people sent over 65 *billion* e-mails to each other. If you factor
in the all the spam messages being generated by netbots and regular flesh-and-blood creeps, the volume is exponentially higher: 2
million e-mails a second, 171 billion every day![2] Even a former English major like me can do the math: Using only the number of "real"
e-mails created in 2006, we created an average of ten e-mail messages for every man, woman and child on earth. Even when we write
other kinds of documents—a project summary, a performance appraisal, a pricing spreadsheet, a proposal—we often deliver them as
attachments to an e-mail. E-Mail is easy, it's usually convenient, and
it's cheap.

E-Mail is so pervasive and necessary that most people maintain
multiple accounts, about three accounts each on average. Nearly
everyone has separate business and personal accounts. And it's not
just the traditional office worker who depends on e-mail. People in the
trades rely on instant messaging and e-mail to communicate with the
home office, customers, and suppliers. It's much simpler for both you
and the exterminator to exchange e-mails confirming an appointment
for next Wednesday morning than to play phone tag. In fact, across the
spectrum of work activities, phone calls are no longer as efficient or
convenient as sending or receiving an e-mail or a text message.

Other modes of business writing are still important, of course.
We need to write proposals to convince other people to adopt our
recommendations. We deliver project summaries to keep our clients
informed of progress and to alert them to problems. We write letters
and other documents to announce new products, special pricing,
personnel changes, and other significant events. Our colleagues,
suppliers, and customers still ask for our opinions on matters that
matter to them and sometimes want us to express those opinions
rather formally in a report.

The problem is that e-mail evolved in the Wild Wild West atmosphere of the Internet, where breaking established norms was considered a desirable way to add to your cool factor. As a result,
millions of business writers lack reliable guidelines for writing

[2]See Michael Specter, "Damn Spam: The losing war on junk e-mail," *The New
Yorker* (August 6, 2007), pp. 36-41, for a startling account of the problem.

effectively. In fact, in the relentless pursuit of greater efficiency through e-mail, the traditional virtues of business writing— clarity, conciseness, accuracy, and professionalism—have become casualties to progress.

It doesn't have to be that way. We don't have to trade a measure of effectiveness for greater efficiency. We should be able to achieve both. For example, there's no reason people can't get in the habit of writing one way in a business setting and a different way when they are text messaging somebody in their baseball rotisserie league. And there's no reason that otherwise bright, competent people can't learn to follow a few simple principles in letters and e-mail that can help them write more successfully all the time.

Eight Tips for Creating Successful E-Mail

In fact, before we go any further on our journey, I'd like to share some tips that will make your e-mail more effective without making you any less efficient in sending it. These tips may require forming some new habits or resetting some options in your e-mail server, but all of them are simple. Several of these tips are just matters of simple courtesy. Or common sense.

As my friend, Terry Hill, the head of proposal operations at Barclays Bank in London, said (in an e-mail, of course), "The extensive use of e-mails and text messaging has resulted in a generally lazy and poor standard of writing across the world as a whole." Sure seems that way. For some reason, a lot of people just don't try to write clearly, concisely, or correctly when they use e-mail. So here are eight simple tips that can eliminate a boatload of problems.

1. Choose a businesslike e-mail name. Calling yourself <u>Redneck Geezer@gmail.com</u> might be fine if you're exchanging messages only with your buddies. It's a poor choice if you're trying to conduct business. If you work for a business or organization, it probably has a protocol for e-mail accounts, including how your name is set up, so this isn't much of an issue. However, if you're self-employed, it's worth thinking about. Will you be taken seriously if your e-mail messages come from <u>fuzzybear@yahoo.com</u>? And getting a domain name that mirrors your business's name isn't too difficult or very expensive. Your Internet service provider can probably help you with the process. It's worth the effort. Your e-mail is much more likely to be recognized and read if it identifies who you are and where you work: george.stallings @adventcorp.com, for example.

2. Use the subject line. It's foolish not to use the subject line. And it seems a

> *Eight Tips for Better E-Mail*
>
> 1. Choose a businesslike e-mail name.
> 2. Use the subject line.
> 3. Sign your e-mails.
> 4. Avoid writing too informally.
> 5. Limit your use of emoticons and acronyms.
> 6. Be polite.
> 7. Write to be read on the computer.
> 8. Check it before you send it.

little rude, too. When I get a message with nothing in the subject line, even if it's from somebody I recognize, I feel a little irritated. Couldn't they spend five seconds and give me a clue as to why they're writing? Plus, with the huge gush of spam that's gets flushed into our inbox each day, we all need to go through and quickly delete everything that looks suspicious. If I don't immediately recognize your user name, and there's no subject line in your message, there's a very good chance I'll delete it. I'm sure you do the same.

Maybe even more important, the subject line is your first and best chance to help your readers figure out quickly whether they want to read your message. Maybe you think that everyone should read every word of every message you write, but that's just not going to happen, so your second best goal should be to make the reading process as simple and painless as possible and to make your message look relevant and interesting.

A good subject line should be clear, specific, and short. Short is particularly important, because it may get truncated, depending on how your recipients have their e-mail systems configured. They may see only the first half dozen words in the subject line and have to guess from that whether your message is worth reading.

3. Sign your e-mails. Put your name at the end of your message and follow it with your contact information. Your contact information should include your full name if you typically sign your e-mails with a nickname. For example, if you sign them "Meg," you should write "Megan T. O'Brien" afterward. In addition, include your job title, the organization you work for and your telephone number(s) in case the recipient wants or needs to call you. Some people also include their mailing address as part of their signature block.

As you probably know, you can set your e-mail system up to add this information automatically every time you write. Even better, you can set it up to put a different signature block after your messages depending on whether you are authoring a new message or responding to one somebody sent you. In the case of a reply, it seems reasonable to assume that a shorter version of your signature would be adequate—just your name, your organization, and your phone number(s), for example.

4. Avoid writing too informally. One reason e-mails fail is the fact that people tend to write e-mails much more casually and informally than they do business letters or other documents. That informality is possibly a consequence of the T-shirt and flip-flops culture that gave birth to the Internet in the first place, but the fact is it can lead to some embarrassing errors. My guess is that the frequency of misspelled words, grammar mistakes, punctuation errors, and similar goofs is a lot higher in e-mails than it is anywhere else in business communications.

This rule applies to instant messaging and chat systems, too. Many firms now use chat functions at work so employees can ask questions, share ideas, and otherwise communicate with each other. One of my sons, an attorney, regularly uses chat to communicate with other attorneys at his firm, not only in the Los Angeles office, where he works, but across the network with attorneys in New York City. Similarly, his older brother, who is a software architect, lives and works in Boston but is part of a team primarily based in Ohio. As the technology lead for the firm, he has to be available to the other developers all the time, and they use a chat application for that purpose. Chat is likely to be even more informal than e-mails, but when it's too informal it may become distracting or incomprehensible.

Excessive informality leads to another kind of problem, one that affects the tone of our message. When we write too casually, we may sound amateurish or juvenile. For example, I received an e-mail from a woman who was coordinating a Webinar series where I was scheduled to be a presenter in a couple of months. (In case you're not familiar with them, a Webinar is a kind of seminar broadcast over the Internet, where attendees dial in to a toll-free conference bridge or listen via an Internet audio feed and log in to a Web site to watch your slides and listen to you present. Often these sessions are interactive, so attendees can speak or at least write messages to you during your presentation.) Anyway, putting one of these on takes a lot of coordination, which is why the woman was emailing me. Here's her message:

Hi, Tom!

Thank you so much agreeing to be a presenter during our Thought Leaders series! That is so awesome!!! If you could just send your slides to me by the end of next week, that'd be great. Thank you!!!

Amber

Okay, the message was clear enough. Amber wanted my Power-Point file by the end of the following week. No problem. And she certainly seemed enthusiastic about the whole project. You have to give her points for that. But by using eight exclamation points in the space of four lines, Amber has fatally undercut her credibility. In fact, I find myself wondering if she's about 13 years old and temporarily helping out at her parents' office. About the only thing she could have done to damage her credibility further was to put a smiley face after her name.

But wait! I spoke too soon. After the Webinar was over, I got the following message from her:

Hi Tom,

Thank you for a wonderful presentation! Your Webinar was both informative and entertaining!!! ☺

Have a great day!

Amber ☺

Everybody loves compliments, and I'm certainly no exception. But those smiley faces . . . Ugh.

5. Limit your use of emoticons and acronyms. Smiley faces don't belong in your business e-mails. "Emoticons" is the term applied to the various combinations of punctuation used to express emotion and to the actual icons that show little faces in various states of happiness or distress. For example, **: -)** indicates happiness, while **: - O** is supposed to suggest surprise. Using these things is all right if you're sending an e-mail to a good friend, to a child, or to a message board, such as one where you can anonymously post your feelings about your favorite sports team. If you want to show that the quarterback's performance in last week's game made you feel sick, go ahead and stick in the green, queasy-looking face. But no emoticons in your business e-mails, please. They're inappropriate.

The same goes for cryptic abbreviations and acronyms. Recently a colleague of mine in the U.K. sent me an e-mail in which he wrote,

---

The client would like you to pencil in the last two weeks of September, if possible, to run another program for them. Can you as a first step, let me know WRT September?

I let him know which dates in September were open, but I had to ask him what did he mean by "WRT." I felt a little stupid, but I couldn't figure it out. He wrote back:

WRT: With Respect To!

Okay. Now I felt really dumb. But at least I knew what the acronym meant.

What if I hadn't been a good friend and colleague, but rather a customer. Would I have asked for a definition? Probably not.

What about your business or professional correspondents? Are you certain they all know what LOL means? What about IMHO? Or YMMV? How about FMI? AFAIK?[3]

If you do a lot of instant messaging or hang out on MySpace, you're probably rolling your eyes at me. These acronyms are the lingua franca of the online world, a staple of the vocabulary of the IM crowd. But I have to confess that for quite a while I thought LOL meant "lots of luck." As a result, I often couldn't quite grasp what the writer was trying to say by using that term. Were they being ironic? Sarcastic? Imagine my surprise to learn it actually means "laugh out loud." Needless to say, I didn't LOL.

(If you're as clueless as I am about most of these acronyms, you can find a helpful list of definitions for Internet acronyms on Wikipedia at http://en.wikipedia.org/wiki/FFO#W.)

6. Be polite. At the opposite end of the spectrum from the excessive chumminess and breathless excitement that we see in some e-mails, there's the problem of rudeness. Some people are so tone deaf to the sound of their own language that they don't realize their messages sound rude. Other people just don't care. Either way, it's inexcusable.

"Flaming" was a common problem in the early days of the Internet. Flaming is the act of attacking another person, his ideas and opinions, his lineage, his sexual orientation, and anything else you can think of throwing in the mix, often in obscene or foul language. These messages are usually written by cowardly little nerds who would never have the courage to say anything like that to another person's face. However, they seem to have a lot of courage when they can write anonymously on some Web forum. Flaming seems to have died down a lot in recent years. That's good. The World Wide Web needs all the civility we can muster.

The problem with rudeness is subtler than flaming someone. Occasionally people write e-mails in the heat of strong emotion—anger, disgust, fear—and those emotions lurk in the tone of the message.

---

[3]If you're like me, you'll need to have these defined. IMHO is "in my humble opinion." YMMV means "your mileage may vary." FMI means "for my information" or "for more information" depending on which acronym list you check. And AFAIK stands for "as far as I know." At least AFAIK it does.

Other people just don't seem to realize they're coming across as obnoxious or arrogant or demanding. Perhaps both of those factors played in to the Cerner Corporation memo that we looked at earlier. Here's a more typical example of the kind of thing we see all the time:

All,

Once again one of you has asked to have the schedule changed for the upcoming review session. This is NOT an option. Scheduling the room and equipment is not easy, and rescheduling it once was even harder. At this point, you just need to show up and do your part. And please don't think scheduling problems give any of you an excuse to skip the review. That is not going to happen.

Dorothy

Maybe Dorothy has reached the breaking point on this issue, but regardless, she comes across as petulant and rude. Putting something in print tends to exaggerate the extreme elements of any tone it may have, so when it comes to strong emotions in an e-mail, less is definitely more. If you're angry, upset, or in the grip of some other strong emotion, wait before writing. Then, after you've cooled down a bit, write your message so that you wouldn't mind having it read out loud in front of your mother. Or your boss. Or printed on the front page of the *New York Times*.

7. Write to be read on the computer. On a flight I was taking a few months ago I noticed the woman across the aisle from me take out a thick sheaf of papers from her briefcase. It was obvious from the formatting that they were e-mails she had printed out. Intrigued, I watched her for a few minutes. She put the stack on the tray table in front of her and attacked them, pen in hand. Most of them she simply skimmed quickly, then drew a line through. On a few she scrawled some comments at the bottom of the page. As she finished each page, she tucked it under the stack and kept on moving.

Her behavior was unusual, but it wasn't hard to figure out why she was doing this. Many people don't enjoy reading text on a computer screen. Screen resolutions are less than perfect, so type is less readable on a screen than it is on paper. Computers are bulkier and harder to handle than a stack of paper. And, most important, documents are harder to skim when they appear on a screen.

Why does this matter? Because most business people prefer to skim the documents they get. In fact, research indicates most people never read an entire document from front to back. Instead, they usually glance at the opening paragraphs, turn to the back of the document to look for a conclusion, summary, next steps, price, or similar information, and then flip back and forth through the rest, absorbing the gist of it by skimming. Obviously, it's much easier to skim text when you can hold actual pages in your hands and let your eyes roam over the entire document.

Another problem that detracts from readability with e-mail is the lack or loss of formatting. For example, with a little forethought you can help the reader grasp your key points quickly by using headings, subheadings, indentations, bullet points, enumeration, and other formatting tricks that make the text on the monitor a little easier to skim. But given the current state of the art, you can't reliably do that in e-mail. Some e-mail servers strip out formatting elements. Even if you create your e-mails in a mark-up language, such as HTML, there's no guarantee your recipient's computer can decode it. Even if you write within the word processor and then paste that message into your e-mail, your recipient may still receive nothing more than stripped-down plain text. In my own experience, this problem seems to happen more often when I am responding to a message that was sent to me by somebody using a handheld device. But it can even occur when you are composing a new message.

I received the following e-mail from a person I had never met or spoken with before. What kind of impression do you think it made on me?

Tom,

I would like to offer you my services as a writer. I often write on free-lance assignment for organizations in various industries either under my name or as a ghost writer. I'm known for my industry white papers, but I have also been engaged for marketing collateral, presentations, application briefs and web content. <!—[endif]—>

I believe I can provide you with a unique writing resource and perspective. I'd be pleased to explore the possibilities. <!—[if !support-EmptyParas]—><!—[if !supportEmptyParas]—> Would you like to set a time in the next week or so for a brief conf. call to discuss?

I think there are a lot of things wrong with that e-mail, but the sudden intrusion of broken HTML code definitely made me doubt his skill as a business or technical writer. I've tried to figure out what on earth was going on there, and my best guess is that this was a generic e-mail containing merge codes that he sent out to a lot of people and the process had broken without his realizing it. (By the way, the other problems with this e-mail, in my opinion, are the abrupt salutation from a total stranger ["Tom,"], the lack of focus on what kind of writing I or my company might need [we don't need white papers], the lack of conviction in his claim ["I believe I can provide you. . . "], the odd decision to describe himself as "unique" rather than "experienced," "professional," or "successful," the equally odd way he separates himself from the recommendation by saying he will "provide" a "resource," rather than saying he will do the work himself, and the sudden clipped tone at the end—". . . for a brief conf. call to discuss.")

Bear in mind that if you are composing in HTML or a rich text format (RTF), your message may look wonderful on your screen, only to arrive at your recipient's computer looking even worse than the example above. That will happen if your recipient doesn't have an HTML or RTF compatible system or simply has those functions turned off. Such basic niceties as indentations, fonts, italics, bold face, bullet points, and so forth will all disappear. What my correspondent, quoted above, was trying to do is fairly sophisticated—he was creating some kind of merge document that failed to merge correctly. But what you and I typically try to do in our e-mails, simply writing a coherent message, may also involve using code that won't translate to your recipients' screens. In-

Formatting E-Mail

1. Use Rich Text Format but don't depend on your format holding.
2. Write with a clear logical pattern.
3. Use obvious transition words.
4. Avoid garish formatting choices, including "stationery" and fancy fonts.

stead, what they see is an undifferentiated mass of Courier. That's why it's so important in e-mails to get the internal logic of the message right, in case the surface appearance—the formatting—disappears. My recommendation is to write in rich text format (RTF), but to make sure the message is organized so that the ideas flow logically. Also, use verbal cues to structure ("First,..." "Second,..." "On the other hand,..." "Finally,..."), because those won't be wiped out if your message gets reduced to plain text.

And while we're on the subject of formatting, may I humbly suggest that you resist the urge to decorate your e-mails by using backgrounds, colors, and fancy typefaces? Some e-mail systems give you the option of choosing a "stationery" style—colors, patterns, grid lines, and so forth. These options invariably make your messages look amateurish and often make them harder to read. I regularly get business e-mails from someone who has chosen to use a blue background that is supposed to suggest a cheerful sky, I guess, and then prints the message in dark blue letters over that. The combination definitely does not enhance the message's readability or the author's professionalism.

8. Check it before you send it. If the message matters, write it and edit it outside your e-mail system. The temptation to write an e-mail inside Outlook or Notes or whatever e-mail system you use is almost irresistible. Usually it doesn't matter. Even though we know that we're more likely to make mistakes and that the editing tools in our e-mail system are only a subset of what we have in our word processor, we opt for convenience rather than caution.

That's fine most of the time. But when your e-mail message really matters, you're better off composing it in your word processor, editing it there, getting it right, and then copying and pasting it into the message space of your e-mail system. You're a little more likely to catch the typos, misspelled words, and other mechanical problems that way.

Moving Beyond the Mechanical

Of course, mechanical errors, misspelled words, grammar mistakes, and typos are actually the least of our worries. If your writing is riddled with those kinds of errors, you'll distract and possibly annoy your reader, and you'll certainly damage your credibility. But these mistakes are not the ones that cause the most costly damage. If you look back at those two disastrous e-mails written by company CEOs, neither one of them had misspelled words and neither one of them contained typos. The grammar was fine, too, even including their use of sentence fragments to create an individual tone. No, the real problems lay much deeper. They failed to accomplish their supposed purposes—inspiring, motivating, setting a vision for the future. And they created much larger problems for their authors and the companies they headed than they were trying to fix.

In this book, we will move beyond the merely mechanical errors—the punctuation mistakes, misspelled words, and grammar goofs that everyone makes from time to time. Rather, our focus will be on writing effectively. The purpose of this book is to provide some guidelines for business writers who want to feel confident that the e-mails, letters, and other documents they write are successful in making a clear point, communicating a credible opinion, effectively motivating others, or even persuading the reader to adopt a particular point of view.

> *Words to Write By . . .*
>
> Effective writing does not depend on correct grammar and spelling. It depends on sound thinking, an understanding of the audience, and a clear sense of your purpose in writing.

What the book won't do is tell you how to install a spam filter, how to set up multiple e-mail accounts for your office, or how to launch an e-mail marketing campaign. That kind of technical information is beyond my limited domain of expertise. The book also will not attempt to deal with the human resource and legal issues involved in writing a performance appraisal, the contractual issues inherent in a proposal, and so on. Technical tasks and the legal implication of your writing are topics best left to the techies and the lawyers respectively. Instead, my goal is to outline how you can write clearly and effectively. I will show you some simple techniques that will enable you to communicate as professionally as possible. Knowing these techniques will save you and your reader time and effort, will prevent errors and misunderstandings, and will help you create a favorable impression. Sloppy, unclear, incomprehensible writing suggests that the person who produced it is incapable of thinking clearly or producing high quality work. That's not fair—you may believe that your skills as a civil engineer or an investment advisor or a purchasing agent or whatever you do professionally have very little to do with your ability to write well—but nobody ever said life would be fair. The fact is it's in your best interest to learn how to communicate effectively, to learn how to use the language of success.

In the next chapter, *The Problem,* I'll sketch the typical mistakes people make in writing e-mails, letters, and other documents. Specifically, I'll describe four "languages" people use that simply don't work: Fluff, Guff, Geek, and Weasel. Each of these languages fails in business communications because each makes it difficult for the reader to understand the message. These languages often create the wrong impression, they can undercut rapport between sender and receiver, and they may diminish the writer's professionalism and credibility. The use of these ineffective languages is often a matter of bad habits. By pointing out their characteristics and how to revise them, I hope to make you hypersensitive to these four faulty languages. I will have accomplished my

Words to Write By . . .

People judge you and get to know you through your writing.

purpose if you cringe a little when you see someone else writing in one of those modes, and if you self-censor to eliminate them from your own work.

Of course, anybody can point out problems. Even if I've managed to define the problem in a way that's different and helpful, the real reason you're interested in this book is that you're hoping to see some answers. I provide those in Chapter 3, *The Principles*. There I discuss the "language of success," a language characterized by five principles. Effective business writing of any form, from e-mails and letters to complex proposals and manuals, must be clear, concise, precise, suited to its audience, and suited to its purpose. I give you examples of what it takes to write clearly, how to write more concisely, what kinds of precision matter, and what it means for a document to be suited to its audience and its purpose.

To that end, Chapter 4, *The Practice,* shows how to apply the right structural pattern as determined by document purpose. In that chapter, I'll show you how each of the main reasons we write in a business or organizational setting—to inform, to evaluate, to motivate, and to persuade—requires a unique structural pattern. Then I'll show you how the pattern for each purpose can be adapted to create specific kinds of documents within that category. Although many of the samples I provide are formatted as e-mails, since that's what people write more often than any other kind of document, I also include other types of business writing, providing examples of reports and letters that you may need to write. I hope the samples will be instructive and useful for you, naturally, but ultimately no matter how many samples I put in a book like this, there will never be enough because each writing situation is unique. I firmly believe it's far more important for you to understand how to create your own successful documents. Simply copying somebody else's version of a "complaint letter" doesn't really teach you how to do the next one on your own. In the long run, you'll be a more effective writer if you understand the logic that makes writing work. Then you'll have the power to communicate effectively in your own voice. You'll be fluent in the language of success.

Finally, a quick note on the examples that appear in the book: They are based on real writing that I've collected from a wide variety of sources over the years. I've modified the examples to protect the author and—well, let's be honest here—to protect myself, too, since nobody wants to be told that her e-mails were ugly or incompetent. In a few cases, to illustrate a particular point, I've made up an example, too. In every instance, I have made up names for writers, recipients, companies, organizations, departments, agencies, products, services, and so on. They're all fake. So are the locations, timelines, pricing, specifications, and other details contained in the various examples, good and bad. They're all just little works of fiction. So if you happen to see the name of a person you know or of a company you think you might have heard of, forget about it. It's just an unfortunate coincidence.

CHAPTER 2

The Problem

How Fluff, Guff, Geek, and Weasel Ruin Your Writing

Language: The Medium of Business

We live in language the way dolphins live in water. Language is such a fundamental aspect of the experience of being human that we become oblivious to it. Yet it has a profound effect on every aspect of our life. We connect with other people, establish rapport, share emotions, communicate ideas, propose solutions, inspire, instruct, chastise, praise, seduce, worship: *all in and through language*. Language facilitates the most fundamental of human activities. In our professional lives, our skill in using language to accomplish these activities will contribute to our success or failure. Words embody ideas and feelings. Sentences give shape to our thoughts and make things happen. And written language is usually the vehicle by which we communicate our most important messages. We know, of course, that nonverbal means of communication matter. An angry glance from our lover, a wide smile on the face of our child, a client who sits impassively behind the desk, arms folded: We don't really need words to get the message. But when it comes to more complex messages, words are indispensable. And in modern business, written words are the most indispensable of all.

Unfortunately, there's a problem. People struggle to write messages that are clear and concise. In that struggle they often lose their own voice, sacrifice their own authenticity, and produce writing that ultimately betrays them and their readers. They hate to write and the results typically reflect that fact.

Why does this happen? Well, the popular answer is that our education system is doing a bad job of preparing young people for the world of work. That failure supposedly includes inadequate or incompetent instruction in the skill of writing. People in every English-speaking nation in the world have earnestly confided in me that the education system in their country is broken and desperately needs to be fixed, because "nobody knows how to write any more." It's an easy answer, but I doubt that it's the full truth. In my experience, teachers at all levels of the educational system, from preschools to postgraduate courses, embrace the notion that students must learn to express themselves clearly and concisely. They require more writing of their students now than they have at any time in the past fifty years or so. Critical thinking is a core component of every major I know anything about, including fields that traditionally have minimized writing, like engineering and mathematics. In general, students are getting more practice in writing and more feedback from their instructors about their writing than their parents or their grandparents ever did.

> *Words to Write By ...*
>
> If you write clearly, people assume you think clearly.

Even in the best educational environments the kind of writing we do as part of our coursework is nothing like the kind of writing we need to do once we enter the world of work. That dissimilarity is the root of the problem. If our English comp instructor has assigned us to write a two-page essay about a short story or a poem, we don't learn in the process of doing the assignment how to analyze our writing tasks in terms of their purpose. We don't learn to adapt our writing to meet the requirements of different audiences. And we don't acquire the fluency to write in a professional tone that still sounds unmistakably like us. The assignment is artificial by nature and so is the writing we produce in response to it.

When we actually start work, we have little to no experience in writing appropriately on the job. Instead, we tend to copy what others have produced—which typically means copying somebody else's bad example. We adopt an artificial tone that presumably sounds smart or professional, but is actually more likely to sound stilted or awkward. In short, we begin to communicate in languages that don't work.

I have worked with thousands of business professionals all over the world, helping them articulate important messages about their businesses, their products, their solutions, their innovations, and their goals for the future. I'll admit that I've occasionally been frustrated by the apparent inability of well-educated people to communicate their ideas clearly. But I've also been gratified and humbled to see people who had struggled to express themselves adopt a few basic techniques, practice them, and develop a capacity for writing well that they never dreamed they possessed. From these experiences, I've come to believe that good writing is a skill, one that can be learned. Just a few basic principles, when followed intelligently, can help business and technical professionals communicate more successfully. Raising these principles to a level of conscious awareness ultimately helps a writer do a better job.

The Language of Success

I've bandied about the title of this book, *The Language of Success*, but I haven't defined it yet. So what is the language of success? In a phrase, it's language that works. The word "success" specifically refers to whether a given message successfully fulfills the goal for which it was created. The language of success succeeds, in other words, because it transfers information clearly and quickly so that another person can use that information to do his or her job. Or because it expresses our opinions in a way that sounds reasonable and justified, so that we appear to be a person whose opinion actually matters. It succeeds because it's language that cuts through the clutter of commercial and marketing hype to deliver a persuasive message, enabling our customers to see that what we offer is a sensible solution to meeting their needs, solving their problems, strengthening their own organizations, and obtaining superior value in the process. The language of success is writing that works for a living. It's writing that makes a point and ultimately makes a difference.

But the language of success is also a way of expressing yourself so that people see *your* true value. The success in this sense refers to your own growth, your career development, and your influence. If you learn to write clearly and concisely, your colleagues and customers will see you as a competent professional. We all assume that writing mirrors thinking. Bad writing suggests sloppy thinking. Good writing suggests clear thinking. If you can write effectively about a particular subject, we assume you understand that subject. We start to view you as an authority on the topic. By writing clearly, you are seen as someone who is credible. Other people are more likely to trust you.

There's a third dimension to the language of success. It's the fact that we tend to assume that writing reveals character or a writer's true intentions. If someone writes in a stilted, pompous style, we suspect he is actually insecure and doesn't trust us to take his information seriously. If people use flowery language or waffle constantly, refusing to make a point directly, we may think they are trying to bamboozle us. For example, the real damage done by those two disastrous e-mails from CEOs was not in misleading employees about what work needed to be done or how managers should set their priorities. The real damage, I think, came from the fact that you can't read those e-mails without coming to a rather damning conclusion about the characters of the individuals who wrote them. That may not be fair. Perhaps both of these men were having very bad days and experienced the kind of meltdown we've all gone through from time to time. Perhaps it's just bad luck that they happened to record their meltdowns in print and e-mail them to their employees. But fair or not, we tend to judge people as people by the way they write. We often do it unconsciously, but we definitely do it.

In using the language of success you should have a unique voice. Your writing should sound like you. Too often, however, we lapse into artificial voices that don't sound like us at all. We imitate languages that are used all around us. In fact, they are so pervasive that

> *Words to Write By . . .*
>
> If you write clearly, you'll be viewed as credible and trustworthy.

a young person who is fairly new in the workplace may conclude these languages are the "correct" way to write in business. To a veteran with many years of experience, these odd ways of writing may no longer sound so odd. Like an annoying whine in the air conditioning unit, like a constant pounding in the plumbing, like brakes that squeal whenever we press the pedal, after a while the irritating grate and clunk and rasp of these languages may fade into the background. However, they still create strain. They still interfere with effective communication. They are still nonfunctional. And it's worth the effort to eliminate them.

Four Languages That Don't Work

Stay alert and you'll start to notice four of these nonfunctional languages that pop up all the time. I call them Fluff, Guff, Geek, and Weasel. These are languages of failure, not success. These are languages that you definitely don't want to use. Unfortunately, we're immersed in them, and if you imitate what you get in your own e-mail inbox without thinking, you'll find that you lapse into them unaware.

Fluff

Fluff is the language of grandiose claims, vague assertions, and hype. We see this kind of language in marketing materials, on corporate Web sites, in proposals and sales letters. But it's so insidious, it can creep into our ordinary writing style.

I recently started working with a new client, so one of the things I did to get ready for our first meeting was to visit the Web site. It was not a good experience. The site was well designed, it had nice graphics, and it was easy to navigate. So what's the problem? The words. Everything that was written about the services consisted of dull, worn-out clichés— "leading edge," "state of the art," "innovative," even

The Characteristics of Fluff

1. Cliché expressions.
2. Grandiose claims.
3. Minimal or no evidence.

that bloated loser "synergistic." Yikes! The client's messages were vague and not the least bit persuasive.

Most sales and marketing professionals want to write clearly, concisely, and persuasively. Unfortunately, in spite of good intentions, they often produce writing that is muddled, wordy, and unconvincing. However, it's never too late to learn, and the potential payback is huge. Research indicates that if you send your prospects clear, concise, and persuasive e-mails, letters, and proposals, you can shorten your sales cycles by more than a third. Even if your job isn't directly involved in sales, avoiding fluff will help you create a better impression and gain more respect and influence within your organization.

Here's another example, an e-mail sent to a prospect that relies on vague language and grandiose claims but doesn't really say anything:

Subject: Your inquiry

Dear Mr. Brown,

Thank you for your inquiry.

As you may know, Wilcox DataFlex Inc. is uniquely qualified to deliver world-class results. We offer best-of-breed products and customer-focused service to produce seamless solutions. Our commitment to partnering with our customers produces innovative yet user-friendly applications.

I look forward to discussing our applications with you to see if there's a good fit. Please let me know a time that will work for you.

Regards,

Stacie

Sound impressive? No, not really. In fact, this paragraph is likely to start the client's built-in B.S. detector clanging like a fire alarm.

Why doesn't it work? What makes this kind of language sound weak and phony? The problem comes from making big claims unsupported by even a sliver of proof. *World-class results?* Says who? *Best-of-breed products?* By what standards? *Seamless?* So what does that even mean?

To get rid of fluff, we need to back up our claims with details. Suppose the e-mail had been written as follows:

Subject: Your inquiry about DataFlex imaging systems

Dear Mr. Brown,

Thank you for your inquiry. On the Web form you completed, you indicated an interest in our imaging systems.

Besides the actual features of our products, there are two important differentiators that have made us the right choice for many banks around the world and that may be important to you:

First, Wilcox DataFlex has successfully installed advanced imaging systems in more than 500 financial institutions in North America, more than any other firm in the industry.

Second, we offer the latest technology, including digital scanning, and back our systems with a one-year, unconditional guarantee and a service department that is available 24 hours a day, 7 days a week.

As a result, by choosing us you will achieve three important outcomes: First, your operations will be in full compliance with all federal and state regulations. Second, you will eliminate more than 70% of the paper routinely generated in the course of business. And third, your total cost of operations will go down due to reduced information storage costs. On average, over the past three years, our customers have saved more than $275,000 annually.

We can determine if DataFlex will deliver those results for you in about ten minutes. All we need to do is explore three simple questions when we talk. Are you available for a brief phone call next Monday, before noon? And would you like me to also arrange a Web-based demo of our system so you can see it in action? Let me know if next Monday works for you.

Regards,

Stacie Alexander

The second version is a more effective message, isn't it? If you got it, instead of the first one, you'd be a bit more impressed, right? It's all in the details. If you can make big claims, make them. But back them up with evidence. Don't let them float untethered on the page like giant bags of hot air.

Here are some examples of words and phrases typical of Fluff. Does anything look familiar here?

- Best of breed
- Compelling
- World class
- Leading edge
- State of the art
- Quality focused
- Uniquely qualified
- Innovative

- High performance
- Commitment to excellence
- Synergy
- User friendly
- Integrated
- Partnership
- Seamless
- Robust

Why do people write in Fluff? Lack of time, maybe. It can be hard to find good proof to back up assertions we believe are self-evident anyway. So the temptation is to just go ahead and make our claims on the assumption that the reader will agree. Don't do it. It doesn't work.

Another reason people write in Fluff is that they see lots of examples of it all around them. This is the language of the radio ad, the TV commercial, the marketing brochure. We're bombarded with this kind of language on a daily basis, so it's no wonder we start to imitate it.

The very fact that we're bombarded with it, though, makes it particularly dangerous. If you write in Fluff, your reader may become skeptical of what you're saying. After all, if you sound like a shill, your reader may assume you are a shill. Why should I believe you when everything is "world class," "leading edge," "seamless," "robust," "uniquely qualified," and on and on?

Guff
Guff is the language of the bureaucrat. It's needlessly complex, pompous, and dense. The writer proficient in Guff writes long, long sentences, uses big words, including undefined technical terms, and constructs his or her sentences in passive voice. As a result, reading

this kind of writing is akin to slogging through a swamp where the mud sucks at your boots with every step you take.

George Orwell attacked this kind of writing in a famous essay, "Politics and the English Language." He argued that political language is "designed to make lies sound truthful and murder respectable, and to give an appearance of solidity to pure wind." Orwell's agenda had more to do with politics than with clear writing, but his points are valid even if we're not discussing foreign policy. As he saw it, most political speech and writing was "the defense of the indefensible," which required circumlocution, euphemisms, and vagueness. "Defenseless villages are bombarded from the air, the inhabitants driven out into the countryside, the cattle machine-gunned, the huts set on fire with incendiary bullets: this is called pacification," Orwell wrote, and we wince to see how little things have changed.

But it's not just politicians who pump out this kind of smoke screen. Anyone who has an uncomfortable message to deliver is prone to lapse into Guff. For example, consider the fine people who cobbled together the "on board safety briefing" that we've all more-or-less listened to as the aircraft we're strapped into trundles down the runway toward takeoff. The briefing is a classic example of Guff. By using odd language and weirdly abstract expressions, the flight attendant can give us information supposedly intended to make us safer without forcing us to look too closely at the reality behind the words. Let's face it: We are belted into a slender metal tube that will soon be blitzing through the upper atmosphere, where temper-

> *The Characteristics of Guff*
>
> 1. Complex words instead of simple ones.
> 2. Long, complicated sentence patterns.
> 3. Overuse of passive voice.

atures are so cold and oxygen is so scarce that a breach in the skin of that metal tube will mean instant death for all of us. If something horrible should happen at a lower altitude, we still face the prospect of slamming into the earth at speeds approaching those of a bullet. And if we manage to avoid hitting the ground at breakneck speed— "breakneck" indeed; there's an appropriate use of a cliché!—we still face the prospect, particularly on an overseas flights, of crashing somewhere in a large body of water. But never fear: "In a case of a water landing, our seat cushion may be used as a flotation device." Say what?! A water landing? A flotation device?

This kind of language has crept into other aspects of their routine briefing. Now they don't just tell us to turn our electronic gear off. No, they tell us to "put it in the off position." And they don't tell us that we'll exit from the front door. No, we'll be "de-planing" from the "forward cabin" door.

In general, we are far more likely to encounter Guff in writing than we are in speech. The HR department lapses into Guff to tell us about the changes to our healthcare benefits. The engineering group uses Guff to give us a status update on its project. Senior management thinks that explaining the coming year's objectives in Guff will somehow make them sound more impressive. They talk about "achieving traction" in the market, about "increasing our bandwidth" (by which they mean "awareness," not network capacity), about "leveraging" opportunities, resources, ideas, and all kinds of other stuff, and about "expanding mindshare." All of these people think they are communicating in a powerful way. But they're wrong. Wrong every time. Instead what they are writing sounds like B.S. It sounds like someone who is trying to defend the indefensible.

Here's a dandy example of a simple idea written in Guff:

> The dimensionality of expected project problems coupled with the limited time available for preparation means that choices will have to be made to assure viability of the most critical analytical processes. Thus, a leveraging of problem similarities and process relationships to allow sharing of resources and solutions, will be needed to contain cost and staff expenditures and assure maximum payoff from effected solutions.

I'd be willing to bet that when you saw the word "dimensionality," you knew we were in trouble with this one. Right? And when you saw the word "Thus" you probably felt like laughing. *Thus…? Thus* what?

This writing is incomprehensible because the sentences are too long, they are poorly constructed, and the writer has used too many big words. The first sentence is 31 words long. Just as a point of reference, 15 to 17 words is a good average sentence length for educated adults—the kind of people who read *The Wall Street Journal* and *The New Yorker* and your e-mails and other documents. So that first sentence is about twice as long as we'd like it to be. And just in case we thought the author of this jewel couldn't do another sentence like that, he or she comes at us with the second sentence, which is 32 words long.

Okay, so if you translate this passage out of Guff and into successful language, what does it mean? Any guesses?

Well, I confess I'm not sure but I think the writer was trying to say something like this:

> We're facing some big problems on this project and there's not much time to get ready. Making the right decisions at the outset will be vital. I recommend that we look for problems that are similar to each other and for processes that affect multiple parts of the business. That way, the solutions we develop will have the broadest possible impact, and we'll be able to keep staff and expense levels under control.

Again, I'm only guessing. But even if I'm wrong, at least this revised version has the virtue of being comprehensible.

Here's another example of Guff:

> Nova, Inc. has been an industry leader in strategic business programs related to the interaction of the needs of our customers and our philosophies towards **Total Quality Management.** Our goal is to be able to provide a business program that meets two specific criteria.
>
> A. To meet the business requirements of the customer by providing complete flexibility, the highest level of customer service and responsiveness, decreased operating expense, increased profit and,
>
> B. To provide a financial benefit to Nova which will assure Nova's ability to be a long-term business partner

This isn't horrible. It just sounds stiff and pompous. And it's completely inappropriate to the audience, because this chunk of text appeared in a proposal, a document intended for customers, not employees. As you probably noticed, what it literally says is that in the area of quality management, we *would like to have* a program that does two things. That's our *goal*. Apparently we're not there yet. We don't actually have a QC program, but, hey, a company has to have a dream, right? We even have criteria to guide us in selecting a program that will achieve our goal. First, we want to make our customers happy by giving them good service while also cutting our costs and increasing our profits. (Wait a minute—is that really what we want to be saying to the *customer*?) Second, we're interested in a quality program that will enable us to make a lot of money so that we're sure to be around for a long time. In other words, when you strip the language down to an everyday form of expression, we're saying something to a potential client that is actually quite self-serving.

But that's one of the reasons for using Guff. It's a way of saying something so obscurely that (we hope) the reader doesn't actually notice what we've just said. Whether we're defending the indefensible or just covering up the lack of a basic quality control program, we're using pompous language, complex sentences, and big words the way a magician uses misdirection.

Geek

Geek is language that's too technical or too obscure for the intended reader. People use Geek when they don't take the time to think about the reader. They don't stop to consider whether the person who will receive this message has the same background, the same level of technical expertise, the same vocabulary even, as the writer. Lazy writers, the ones who use Geek all the time, don't bother to think about the reader. Instead, they write to the only audience who really matters to them: themselves. They use all of the jargon, acronyms, and cryptic references that only someone as knowledgeable of the subject as they are could possibly understand. And unlike Guff, the use of Geek is not limited to writing. You're quite likely to hear someone using Geek conversationally or in a presentation, too.

We encounter Geek all the time. Recently my 85-year-old mother needed to

The Characteristics of Geek

1. Disregard for the audience's needs.
2. Overuse of jargon and acronyms.
3. A focus on technical details instead of functions or outcomes.

get a new TV set. She wasn't sure what to get, so my wife and I offered to go with her. We normally like shopping at Costco because the prices are cheaper yet the employees are treated well. The problem was that when we looked at the little information cards describing each of the various TV sets, we didn't understand what they meant.

Hmmm. We decided that maybe for this one we needed a salesperson. So we trundled across the parking lot to one of the Big Box electronics stores. We figured we'd still get a good price, and we'd also get some good advice.

After we stood staring at the wall of TVs for a while, a salesperson came over. "You need something?" he asked.

"Mom is interested in getting a new TV," I replied. My mother nodded dutifully.

"Oh, yeah? You want plasma or LCD?"

"What?"

"Plasma or LCD?"

I looked at Mom. She looked at me. We both looked at my wife. We shrugged in unison.

"I don't know. Which is better?"

"Depends. You looking for high def or just HD ready? DLP or ETV? You want six by nine or four by three?"

He stood there with his head cocked to one side, tapping his foot impatiently.

My mother was watching him with a stunned expression on her face. Then she turned to me and in a hurt, somewhat accusatory tone she said, "You didn't tell me there'd be questions. I didn't know there'd be questions."

We tried a different store, but, as Yogi Berra supposedly said, it was pretty much déjà vu all over again. We were in the land of Geek speak, and we didn't understand it. Finally, we just took a chance and bought one that had a good picture in the store and a famous brand name on the front. They said we could bring it back if it didn't work.

The good news is that Mom likes her TV a lot, so everything turned out fine. But it was dumb luck, because we never did find a sales rep who could speak to us in plain English about the options the various makes and models offered and why we should care.

At least in a face-to-face situation like that, we could ask questions and seek clarification. We didn't get much in the way of answers so things didn't get a whole lot clearer, but it could have happened. However, if we had received an e-mail from one of those sales reps, we couldn't even have done that. We'd have been stuck.

Why do people use Geek? Well, when we're communicating with our co-workers, the jargon and the shorthand and the acronyms and the other elements of Geek are actually quite useful. Most of our colleagues understand these terms as well as we do, so talking and writing in that language is actually efficient. Lawyers speak legalese to other lawyers, physicians and nurses speak medicalese to their peers, and so on. Besides the efficiency that comes from speaking in shorthand, it also creates a sense of solidarity within the group and even a little superiority over the uninitiated. We're all part of a select group, because we all understand these terms. We're in with the in crowd.

Okay, fine. So use your jargon with each other. Just don't forget that problems arise when you use that language with us. You do remember us, don't you—*the customers*? The ones who pay your salary?

If you have a job that has its own jargon and acronyms and other elements of Geek in it, try observing what happens when you get home after a challenging day. Let's say that you work as an information technology specialist and you've spent a grueling day porting a client's customer data out of one software application, a database that was installed on a server in her office, and onto another software application, this time one that resides somewhere on the Web and is available as a subscription service. And in the process, you had to preserve certain embedded information and triggers. Not the easiest job in the world, but not the hardest, because this is what you do. When you walk in the door, your significant other beams and says, "Hi, sweetheart. So tell me what you did today." And at that point, your heart probably sinks, because translating what you did into everyday, comprehensible language that your very bright but nontechnical significant other will understand *is* hard work. And it's *not* what you do, at least not normally. At this point in your day, you don't feel like hard work. What you feel like is having a beer. So you just smile back and say, "Oh, nothing really."

To stop using Geek and start using the language of success, we need to develop the flexibility to write at a level that's appropriate for the intended audience. We can't just dump any old Geek on the page and expect the reader to do the work for us. He shouldn't have to. In fact, he probably can't. He can't instantly acquire the in-depth, tacit knowledge that makes Geek comprehensible to those who already understand it. Acquiring that level of fluency takes weeks, maybe months, maybe even years of exposure. Think back to the last time you started a completely new job or even took a similar job at a new company. How many meetings did you sit through, not understanding what your new colleagues were saying? How long did it take before you didn't need to have acronyms clarified?

If you're writing an e-mail message to a client or a prospect, you may be aware that using in-house jargon and acronyms won't work. You're a little less likely to worry about it if you're writing to a colleague. However, if that person works in a different department, she may have no more familiarity with your version of Geek than an outsider. Do you think Dave in Accounting is likely to understand this message from Warren in IT?

Subject: P3 tix for FIMS

Dave,

These are the Prioritized P3 tickets for FIMS. You will note there are the first few prioritized and then the remaining that have not been prioritized but need to be focused on after those prioritized since they have been identified as a higher importance than some of the other p3 tickets in the queue. Please note that there is a question by the BIM as to whether the 3274609 should be an enhancement. I hope to hear on this yet this week.

Warren

No. Probably not.

To avoid using Geek where it's not understood, you might think about your world of work in terms of a series of concentric rings, as in Figure 2.1. You are in the center, master of your domain and of the specialized language that goes with it. There are a few cognoscenti in that inner circle with you, but not many. One level out you have people who recognize some of the more common terms—key bits of technology, product and option names, key processes that you run, stuff like

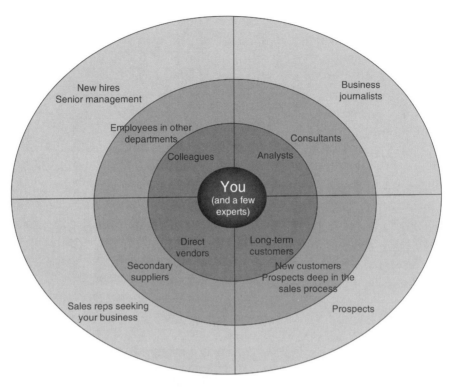

Figure 2.1   Audiences and their familiarity with your jargon.

that. But they don't have any depth behind that recognition. Move out another ring and you have people who have a very basic understanding, They don't recognize the in-house acronyms or jargon, although they might know some of the basic industry terms and concepts. And go another ring out and you've got the mass of people—ordinary, intelligent, reasonably well-educated folks who just happen to be ignorant about your field. You're an accountant and they're civil engineers. You're a pharmacist and they're real estate agents. Whatever. We have to simplify everything down to plain language for these people.

Ignore for a moment that this map of your work life bears a disturbing similarity to Dante's vision of Hell. If there's time, we'll talk about that later. Instead, for now just focus on two facts. First, there are very, very few people who are in that inner circle with you. And, second, we almost always overestimate the other person's level of understanding. The best way to drop the Geek and start using the language of success is to simplify constantly. Remember: If your message is too simple and clear, no real harm is done, but if it's too complex and difficult, you may lose your readers. You might even alienate them. And that's extremely harmful.

Weasel

Weasel is language that sounds wishy-washy, even sneaky. It avoids saying anything definitively. Instead, every assertion is qualified to death. Words and phrases are constantly used to hedge the meaning of what's being said.

Here's an example, where I've put the weasel words and phrases in bold:

Dear Dr. Isawaki,

We **would like** to thank you for the opportunity to submit our proposal. We regard this as a **truly** important project, and **believe** we can add value. For one thing, working with a research organization that has conducted more than 500 global assignments and that has an extensive database of more than 700 university and private sector researchers **would** add significant **value** to this project.

You **can be assured** that we will put our best project management team on this engagement. We **feel very** confident that based on our own internal expertise, the results from the Phase One study and our database of research teams that it **should be possible** to achieve the projected timelines for this project.

In summary, **we believe that** we have proposed an effective solution, based on the information we have **at this time**. We look forward to exploring details of the project at greater depth in the future, but **for now we hope** that this **initial** proposal will **suggest** that there is a compelling case for **considering** us to receive this contract.

Regards,

Cynthia Osgood

Poor Cynthia. She probably believes she's written a persuasive message to Dr. Isawaki. Instead, she's created a message that sounds fawning and weak.

Like the other languages we've discussed, Weasel is a particular combination of vocabulary choices and sentence structures. Specifically, it involves using:

- Weasel words
- Passive voice
- Subjunctive mood

Weasel Words   There are certain "weasel words" that modify the meaning of what you're saying to the point that you appear to be saying one thing when you're actually saying the exact opposite. Weasel words and phrases include "may," "might," "could," "can," "can be," "virtually," "up to," "as much as," "help," "like," "believe," "possibly," and similar qualifiers that create enough wiggle room for a rhino.

Some of the weasel words are qualifiers. They give us protection, "plausible deniability" as they say in Washington. Something "might" happen. Results "may" indicate. It's normal in the course of business to use terms like these, because you don't want to appear to make a commitment you can't keep. (Or your lawyers don't want you to make a commitment that could cause a dispute later on.)

"Our analysis indicates that productivity in the Sheridan facility could increase more than 10 percent once we use the new sequential staging routine in the warehouse." Okay, we honestly believe productivity will go up and our numbers suggest about 10 percent, but let's face it—the warehouse could get hit by a tornado next week and then what happens to productivity? A little caution in the way we say this seems reasonable. We're not trying to mislead anybody.

> *The Characteristics of Weasel*
>
> 1. Hyperqualifying every statement.
> 2. Focusing on "might" and "could" rather than "will" and "can."
> 3. Avoiding responsibility.

Sometimes people use these qualifiers with the deliberate intention of creating a false impression. A few years ago, one of the contenders in the heated battle for enterprise software claimed "100 percent customer satisfaction" in giant headlines in its ads. It was only when you probed into the micro-print at the bottom of the page that you found the qualifications that made that statistic meaningless.

A different kind of problem arises when we start using weasel words all the time, even when there's no need to qualify or soften the assertions we're making. If that kind of language becomes a habit, we create the impression that we're being sneaky. That's not a good move. Or, to put it in Weasel, "we might create the impression that we're possibly being sneaky. That may not be a good move."

Passive Voice   You may have seen the term "passive voice" if you have used the Microsoft Word function that checks your spelling and grammar. The little editing gremlins inside Word put a squiggly line under your verb, and when you right-click on the offending phrase you get a message saying: Passive Voice (consider revising). Okay. But what does that mean? How do we change it? And why is passive voice bad anyway?

To answer the last question first: Nothing is wrong with it in a grammatical sense. It's a perfectly legal way of constructing a sentence in English. But it tends to be harder to decode, and sometimes it's not as clear. As a result, if you use a lot of passive voice constructions, your writing will be harder to read than it has to be.

As for what the term means: "Voice" is simply a bit of grammar jargon that describes the relationship between the subject of a sentence and the verb. In English, we have three different ways to construct sentences based on voice: active, passive, and imperative. In an active voice sentence, the subject *does* the action described by the verb. For example:

> We presented our revised design to the client's architectural review team on Tuesday.

We is the subject of that sentence. And what did *We* do? Well, obviously, We *presented*. But what if we want to put that sentence into passive voice? In a passive voice sentence, the grammatical subject doesn't *do* anything. Instead, it *receives* the action. If we were to flip our sample sentence around into passive voice, we'd write:

> The revised design was presented to the client's architectural review team on Tuesday.

Design is now the subject of the sentence, and the design didn't do anything. It had something happen to it—it *was presented*. It means almost the same thing as the active voice sentence. The difference is one of emphasis. In the first sentence, the focus is on the event—the fact that we presented the design. In the second version, we place emphasis on *what* we presented: The design, not the budget, was presented. Notice, however, that we are no longer as clear about who did the presentation. Passive voice is sometimes confusing about responsibility for an action—which makes it perfect, I suppose, for those writers who are trying to duck responsibility.

We use imperative voice when we are giving an order or providing directions. In an imperative voice sentence, the grammatical subject is left understood—it's *you* who will be doing the action named in the sentence. Here's the same concept in imperative voice:

> Present our revised design to the client's architectural review team on Tuesday.

Now somebody in charge is giving us an order. This definitely has a different meaning than the first two version, because implicitly the presentation hasn't taken place yet. That's why we're being told to do it.

So far, so good. So what's the big deal in using passive voice? Why does it matter? There are two reasons.

First, passive voice inverts the normal word order—the sentence structure that we spontaneously generate about 90 percent of the time and that we hear and read almost as frequently. That lack of familiarity makes it just that little bit harder to decode.

> *Why Passive Voice Doesn't Work*
>
> 1. It inverts the normal relationship between subject and verb.
> 2. It slows down comprehension.
> 3. It sometimes obscures responsibility for action.

Second, as I indicated earlier, if you fail to identify who did the action, a passive voice sentence can be ambiguous, confusing, or even misleading. Here's another example that tilts toward Weasel:

Our purchasing plan provides Sierra Valley Hospital with an opportunity to generate more than $5,000,000 in rebates, shareback, projected cost reductions, and subsidized services/resources that **can be accessed** to reduce supply chain costs while enhancing the service and patient care provided by Sierra Valley.

Can be accessed by whom? Does the vendor do that on behalf of Sierra Valley Hospital? Or does the hospital staff have to do it for themselves? Or does this sentence actually mean that accessing these various cost reduction tools is only hypothetical? That they *can be accessed* under certain circumstances? Hmmm...

Earlier, we had a horrible sample in the Guff category, but part of its incomprehensibility arose from the misuse of passive voice:

...choices will have to be made to assure viability of the most critical analytical processes

All right, choices will have to be made. But by whom? The consultant? Or the client?

Subjunctive Mood   The third element of Weasel is the overuse of *subjunctive mood.* More grammar jargon! But this is pretty easy to understand. When we're talking about something that's true or real, we use *indicative mood:*

As your accountant, I strongly advise you to increase your quarterly withholding amount to avoid facing a serious cash shortage at tax payment time.

If somebody who's not actually our accountant gave us that advice, she might (if she were good at grammar) phrase it in the subjunctive mood:

> If I *were* your accountant, I *would* strongly advise you to increase your quarterly withholding amount to avoid facing a serious cash shortage at tax payment time.

You can see the difference easily enough, I'm sure, but I highlighted the unusual verb forms that put the sentence into subjunctive mood.

We use subjunctive mood to state something that's fictional or hypothetical. The problem—the Weasel element—arises when we use it to state something that shouldn't be hypothetical at all. If we use subjunctive to communicate something that should be a direct statement of fact or opinion, we create confusion.

Some of the ugliest, most notorious examples of Weasel emerge when a public figure has to apologize for bad behavior. President Nixon demonstrated his mastery of Weasel when he resigned the presidency in disgrace. As he left office he said, "I regret deeply any injuries that may have been done in the course of the events that led to this decision. I would say only that if some of my judgments were wrong, and some were wrong, they were made in what I believed at the time to be the best interest of the nation."

The Subjunctive

1. Writing in the subjunctive mood makes every assertion hypothetical.
2. Using the subjunctive mood is like crack cocaine—it quickly becomes an addiction.

Notice first of all that even as he's getting the bum's rush out of the White House, he still doesn't acknowledge that anything he did or authorized to be done caused any injuries. "I deeply regret any injuries *that may have been done…*" That sort of sounds like an apology without actually being one. The latter half of his comments, where he acknowledges that some of his "judgments were wrong," is qualified away into a verbal form of laughing gas when he says that all of his judgments were made "in what I believed at the time to be the best interest of the nation."

Tricky Dick, indeed! But we see equally masterful uses of Weasel among the people we work with every day. Read these sentences and ask yourself: *Do I trust these people?*

> By adopting the radio advertising campaign we have proposed, you may see revenues and market share increase by up to 30 percent or more.

(Yeah, *you may*… Then again, it only happened once. That's why we said "up to." That was the best anybody ever achieved and that might have been a math error, actually.)

> We would like to thank you for allowing us to submit our proposal, which we believe offers significant value-add.

(We would like to thank you, but we had to work all night to finish this thing, so we're not feeling all that grateful. And as for what you *believe,* all I can say is that I still believe in Santa Claus and I still haven't received that pony I asked for, so…)

> Our digital actuators act like the traditional analog variety but are virtually trouble free.

(Kinda like 'em. Quite similar in certain ways. Well, actually, they're totally different, but they pretty much do the same thing. And as for *virtually trouble free,* isn't it true that "virtual reality" isn't real? Close, but no cigar. So how much trouble should I expect if they're *virtually trouble free?*)

Even without my parenthetical sarcasm, you can see that the high quotient of Weasel in those sentences undercuts their credibility.

Why doesn't Weasel work? What makes this writing sound weak and phony? The problems arise from making big claims unsupported by even a sliver of proof. *World-class results?* Says who? *Best-of-breed products?* By what standards? *Seamless?* And what does that mean, anyway? Ask yourself questions like these as you read your own writing and you'll quickly know whether it's Weasel.

Going back to the e-mail message to Dr. Isawaki that we used to start this discussion of Weasel, you can see how many of the sentence are in subjunctive mood or were constructed in passive voice:

We would like to thank you…
…it should be possible to achieve…
…we believe that…

Sadly, this is an example of a writer who uses Weasel words even when they're not necessary. It's probably just a habit for Cynthia, one she's not even aware of. Nor is she likely to realize how weak and ineffective her writing is because of it. If we rewrite Cynthia's e-mail, eliminating all of the unnecessary Weasel, it sounds much more convincing and is a lot easier to read:

Dear Dr. Isawaki,

Thank you for sharing information about your specific requirements. This is an important project, and we are excited to bid on it because we are confident that we can add value. For one thing, we are the only research organization that has conducted more than 500 global assignments and that can draw on an extensive database of more than 700 university and private sector researchers. This combination of experience and resources will save time and money.

We are also confident we can meet the aggressive timelines established for this project. First, as you can see in the Team section of our proposal, we plan to put our most experienced project management personnel on this engagement. As a result, we will be drawing on a deep body of internal expertise, thus shortening the learning curve dramatically for us. Second, we will combine the results we obtained in the Phase One study with our database of research teams to get the project underway quickly.

In summary, we have proposed an effective solution to your need for a global research project in a short time frame. Once we have received your authorization to begin, we will schedule a meeting with you and your colleagues to plan the project in depth. We are eager to start working with you.

Regards,

Cynthia Osgood

Is Clear Writing a Lost Art?

Why do people write poorly? Even more intriguing, why do people, who seem to have little problem communicating clearly when they speak, struggle to make their point when they write?

Clear writing has always been a rare commodity. William Strunk wrote his "little book," *The Elements of Style*, in 1918 because he was dismayed at how poorly Cornell undergraduates wrote. His student, E. B. White, updated it forty years later because he was dismayed at the general lack of clear writing in his day. Now that we're in the twenty-first century, the situation hasn't changed much. Many of the recommendations that Strunk and White made are still helpful. But is it true that the average person's ability to write hasn't improved any in ninety years? Shouldn't we have learned something by now?

It turns out this isn't a simple question. Writing well is a complicated skill. In fact, people are much more likely to speak effectively than they are to write effectively. That's true in the twenty-first century just as it was in the twentieth and just as it has always been. Good writing takes more effort and more conscious insight into the way language works.

One of the core concepts of linguistics is the idea that our brains are structured to produce language as speech and to decode it when we hear it. We define a "dead" language as one that no longer has any native speakers—people who grow up learning the language from its spontaneous use around them. Even if that dead language's written artifacts survive and have an important role in our culture, it's considered dead if it's not spoken.

Writing and reading are secondary or subordinate forms of language production, and they are learned after we have mastered spoken language. This fact explains why little children who are learning to read usually have to say the words out loud and listen to them to figure out what they mean.

> *Words to Write By . . .*
>
> Writing well takes more effort and more conscious insight into the way language works than speaking well does.

Given the primacy of spoken language over written, it's no surprise that people who can speak successfully still have difficulty with writing. Our brains are simply hardwired to produce speech more or less spontaneously. Writing is a different matter. Writing has to be learned consciously, and the process includes a great deal of regularization in terms of standardized spelling, grammar, even word choice, standards that we don't impose on spoken language. We readily accept the fact that people in Boston pronounce words differently than do people in Dallas, but we can't allow them to spell those words differently. Why? Because we need a greater degree of standardization and control in written English to make it work across geographic, cultural, ethnic, and racial boundaries.

As an analogy, consider what happens when analysts working for the CIA or FBI look at a mass of data. Their first goal is to identify patterns within that data that have meaning. The more data they have to look at, the harder it is for them to extract meaning. We do the same thing when we are looking at a written text. By all agreeing to spell words the same way, use the same basic rules of grammar, and so on, we reduce the amount of variation within the data and thereby simplify the process of pattern recognition for ourselves. Written English is actually a subset of the English language, a simplified and regularized and homogenized version in which we can recognize the underlying patterns and from which we can quickly extract meaning. It's still a marvelously complex and rich vehicle for communicating our ideas, opinions, and feelings, but it's less diverse than spoken English.

One source of writing problems, then, stems from our failure to master the rules that simplify and standardize the written system. If you wish to write effectively and clearly, learn to use written English correctly. Use your spelling and grammar checkers. Write shorter sentences. Use the right words in the right way. In short, write clearly and concisely. That is what we discuss in the next chapter.

Some of the rules and guidelines we discuss in the next chapter will dredge up memories of grammar lessons from grade school. Others are tips or tricks that will make your writing sound more professional, even though there's no specific grammar rule behind them.

My goal is to focus your attention on a few things that will help, not to provide a comprehensive guide to all of English grammar and usage. That wouldn't help you much. Instead, you'd probably slide into overload and eventually shut down. From my own ongoing efforts to improve my golf game, I know that if you hear too many tips and techniques and rules and try to think about them all at the same time, you won't be able to hit the ball at all. We don't want that to happen to you as a writer.

To return to the question that opened this section: Is clear writing a lost art? No, I don't think it is. The same skills that made writing work fifty or 100 years ago still work today. And you can develop them so that you write clear, concise, effective e-mails, letters, and other documents every time. You can master the language of success.

CHAPTER 3

The Principles

Modern Methods in Business Writing

Some years ago I was working with a group of chemical engineering majors who were about to be unleashed on the world of work. Someone in the engineering college had noticed that they didn't write very clearly and asked if I could coach them. I worked with them for several weeks, helping them develop skills in writing their reports more clearly and concisely, but not all of the students were thrilled about the program. One of them in particular kept resisting—his assignments were haphazard, his revisions were late, his attitude was apathetic at best. Finally, he reached the point when he just couldn't take my obtuseness any more. "Dr. Sant," he snapped, "I'm sure you mean well and all, but I don't think you get it. You keep trying to get me to be a writer, but that's not what I'm going to do. I'm going to be an engineer. I won't be writing anything!"

It would be fun for me look him up now and ask him if he's written anything lately. But what's the point? We all know the answer.

The reality is most people hate to write and it shows. I'm not sure why they hate it so much, but they do. I suspect part of their dread stems from performance anxiety. It's not that they don't know how to write; it's that they fear doing it poorly and thus embarrassing themselves in front of a group. But, as my former student has probably learned by now, writing is an inescapable part of professional responsibilities.

In the following brief sections, I offer some tips and discuss some modern methods for effective business writing, each focused on a specific principle that will help you write successfully. Whenever possible, I've illustrated the principle with examples drawn from real business writing I've encountered, suitably changed to protect the innocent.

Write the Way You Speak

Earlier I mentioned the fact that most people are more comfortable talking than they are writing, partly because most of us do a lot more speaking than writing, and partly because our brains are hardwired to produce speech. Writing is just a secondary development—a cultural invention—that we have overlaid onto speaking, allowing us to speak at a distance.

Given all that, the advice to "write the way you speak" probably sounds sensible. And to the extent that we use a natural tone and everyday words, thus avoiding Geek and Guff, it's pretty good advice. You can't write exactly the way you speak, of course, because speech is much looser than writing and because we depend heavily on nonverbal tools, such as tone of voice, facial expression, gestures, other forms of body language, and feedback from our audience, to make speech work. None of that is available to us when we write, so we have to work harder to keep our language tight and unambiguous. In addition, spoken language tends to be much more elliptical, full of false starts, pauses, redundancies, and other ephemera that we ignore as listeners but that would drive us crazy as readers. If you've ever obtained the transcript of an interesting interview you heard on TV or radio, you were probably disappointed to read it and see that what sounded focused and smart as you listened seemed elliptical and confused on the page.

We also know that spoken language is by nature much more diverse than the written form of the same language. In creating a diagram of the range of choices available to a speaker or writer, compared to the formality or importance of the situation in which the communication is occurring, you would see that as the situation becomes more formal or important, the range of options narrows.

Figure 3.1 shows that at its roots, down around the base of what looks like a Mayan temple, language is diverse and active and creative. That's where new words are created, arising from slang and from the regional ethnic vocabularies of people who speak in nonstandard ways. As we move into more formal situations, such as writing an e-mail to a client or writing a recommendation letter for a friend, our range of choices narrows. Standard English—the generally accepted grammar and vocabulary that educated speakers are expected to master—becomes the dominant mode. That's true whether we are speaking or writing.

Our habitual speech patterns may not conform to standard usage, particularly if we grew up with a strong regional accent or if we come from a language community where English was not the original tongue. African Americans, Hispanics, Asians, and others tend to have dialect patterns that combine the broad elements of English with other language patterns, creating a unique dialect. Note that there's nothing "wrong" with these forms of English and nothing inherently "right" about standard English. These forms of English are just as "good" and just as valid as Standard English. In fact, within the communities where they are used, they're probably better. After all, the only meaningful test for a language is whether it

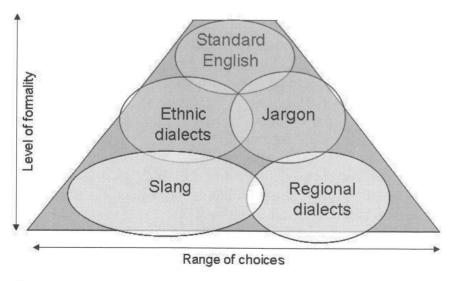

Figure 3.1   The range of options in spoken English.

works. Do the people who use it understand each other? If they do, it's a "good" language.

As we move into the wider world of commerce, however, we have to use language that will be understandable and sound appropriate no matter who is reading our message. By narrowing our choices down to those enclosed within standard usage, we help assure that any listener or reader will understand what we are saying. Thus, if we normally speak in a nonstandard way, taking the advice to write the way you speak could lead to some major problems.

However, there are two areas where trying to write the way we talk can help us—tone and preparation.

The issue of tone of voice in writing is tricky. Some writers have a very distinctive voice. You don't need an advanced degree in literature to recognize the contrast between Henry James, with his complex, highly nuanced writing style, and Ernest Hemingway, the master of the short, direct statement. Each has a unique voice, and each voice is the one that came naturally to him. We can also sound more authentic, more genuine, if we are able to adopt a tone that reflects our style of communicating. Moving down a notch or two on the formality ladder might enable you to avoid some of the worst mistakes in Guff and Geek. Remember: Writing too simply is almost always a better mistake to make than writing too formally. Having fewer barriers between ourselves and our readers is better than having too many.

One way to capture a more authentic tone is to read your writing out loud and listen carefully to how it sounds. Would you actually say it this way? Or have you adopted a false voice? Are you using a language like Geek or Weasel because you're not confident that your normal voice is good enough? Rewrite the parts that sound stilted and false. Delete the jargon, the passive voice, the subjunctive constructions. You can always go back later to make your writing more formal and to check it for conformity to the guidelines of standard English. Breaking the habit of using a false voice is a good first move toward writing more effectively.

The other way in which we can benefit from writing the way we speak is to prepare ourselves to write as carefully as we prepare ourselves to make a speech. How do you react when you are asked to make a formal presentation? If you're like most people, the first thing you probably do is panic. Most of us don't like speaking in public. In fact, more people are afraid of giving a speech than are afraid of spiders or deep water. At some point, though, you get ahold of your emotions and start preparing for the presentation.

Something similar happens when we have to write an important document. We get nervous, we may freeze up a bit, we may abandon faith in our own ability to deliver the message successfully and look for somebody else's material to copy. Those are all normal reactions, but they're not helpful. You need to abandon those behaviors.

One way nervous presenters can calm themselves down is to remember that they don't have to be perfect. They just need to be excellent. Being excellent isn't necessarily easy, of course, but at least it's not impossible. Aiming for perfection means dooming yourself to failure every time. Setting realistic expectations for yourself is an important step along the way to minimizing performance anxiety. This is also true when we write. Nobody writes everything perfectly. Even Shakespeare, according to his contemporary, Ben Jonson, could have erased a lot of lines and done better. Okay, but so what? Even if it wasn't perfect, Shakespeare's stuff achieved such a level of excellence that it still communicates to us today. Our e-mails and project summaries may not have the permanence of Shakespearean dramas, but there's no reason they can't be excellent. And there's no reason we should tie ourselves into knots by demanding more of ourselves than our best.

So how do we achieve excellence? Going back to our comparison to the person who has to give a formal presentation, there are certain steps that increase the likelihood of a successful outcome. If you've had a class in presentation skills, you've probably been told to do follow certain basic steps: Prepare. Relax. Rehearse. The same three steps can help us do a better job when we write, too.

1. **Prepare.** A lot of bad writing is the result of people starting to type before they start to think. Don't write anything until you have a good idea of what you want to say, why you want to say it, and who you're saying it to. If you haven't figured out what you want to say yet, please don't go in search of your message in front of us. Like sausage, business e-mails, letters, and reports

are things we don't want to watch being made. We just want to enjoy the finished product.

2. **Relax.** This doesn't give you permission to be sloppy or careless. But it does give you permission to be yourself. You can use your own voice, rather than one of those stilted pseudo-languages, and you can remind yourself that you almost always make your point when you talk to people. There's no reason you can't do it in writing.

3. **Revise.** If it matters, take the time to get your message right. Just as nobody is good enough to stand before an important group of customers or senior executives and just wing it, nobody is skilled enough to create an important message and just send it out without revising and editing it. Your e-mail program at a minimum probably has spell check and other basic editing tools, but for an important message, you might do yourself a favor to write it in your word processor, work on it until you're happy with it, then paste it into a message block in your e-mail program.

Respect the Medium

As written vehicles for communicating facts, ideas, and opinions, e-mails and letters are related, of course. But there are some important differences between them. Understanding those differences is the first step to handling each of them successfully. If you show some respect for the medium you're using, if you use it the way it was meant to be used, you'll get better results.

For instance, e-mails are frequently sent to a lot of recipients simultaneously. That's very difficult to do with a letter. When you write a letter, you might send copies to one or two other people at most. With an e-mail, you can send it to hundreds. (I'm not including direct mail letters in this, because they're actually advertising documents.)

E-Mails are quick, casual, and convenient. Those are basically good qualities. But those qualities also mean that e-mails usually don't pack a lot of punch. We get so many of them, it's hard to take any particular one seriously. Letters, on the other hand, require composition, printing, and mailing, which means they're a little more work to produce. Plus, their very tactility—the fact that when you get a letter you're really getting something tangible, something you hold in your hands—gives them a bit more importance.

Similarly, it's easy to pass an e-mail on to somebody else. We've all done it. You just click on the button to forward the message, type in the new recipient(s), and hit *send.* Forwarding a letter takes a bit more work. Do you forward the original letter or do make a copy of it first? Do you forward it by mail or do you fax a copy? Or do you scan it into the computer and turn it into an e-mail or e-mail attachment?

Letters are usually a page or two in length, although a letter can easily run several pages long. E-Mails are generally much shorter than that. Letters are usually printed out, but they can be handwritten. In fact, a handwritten letter will communicate a high level of personal commitment or rapport in the right circumstances. E-Mails always appear as text on a screen.

Because a letter is printed on a piece of paper, it's pretty easy to skim. E-Mails, on the other hand, may first appear in a small viewing window that shows only the opening few lines of the message. How much of the message appears depends on how the e-mail system is set up, but it's safe to say that a long e-mail will require your reader to open the message window completely or to use the scroll bar to move through it. In doing so, the reader may be able to skim the contents a bit, but in general, text appearing on a screen is much harder to skim than text on paper. As a result, logical construction is even more important for e-mails than it is for letters. Unfortunately, given the loose, hip, relaxed culture associated with e-mails, logical structure is often lacking.

Similarly, a letter can take advantage of typography to make its key points jump off the page. Bold type, italics, color, different fonts, indentations, white space: All of these can be used in a letter to highlight its contents. You can use some of those same elements in an e-mail, too, but there's no guarantee they'll show up on the recipient's screen. Sometimes formatting is lost. In fact, sometimes even basic characters like the apostrophe are lost, creating some odd-looking monstrosities.

You can send a letter with an attachment, which will almost always consist of another few pages of printed material or another document. Or you might send it with an enclosure, such as a brochure, airline tickets, a packet of flower seeds, a DVD, or pretty much anything else you can shove into an envelope. With e-mail, you can add many of the same kinds of attachments, as long as you can digitize them, plus you can send some things that won't go into an envelope—an audio or video file, for example, a link to a Web site, a spreadsheet, and so on. The flower seeds, however, will be tough.

With e-mails you often have an entire string of messages nested below the most recent one. That way you can retrace the entire sequence of a discussion back to its beginning, although sometimes this nesting becomes lengthy and pointless. Sensible e-mail etiquette suggests deleting the string of previous messages at some point. With a letter, you would almost never include copies of all the previous correspondence unless you were involved in litigation and were enclosing the previous letters for evidentiary purposes.

Finally, there's the issue of formatting. With letters there are some standard formatting practices that everybody follows. For example, your business letter is usually written on letterhead stationery, with your company's logo and other information, such as phone numbers and office locations, prominently displayed. Next, the letter will usually have the date of its composition followed by an inside address, which generally consists of the full name of the recipient (including Mr., Ms., Dr., or other title), the recipient's position, the name of the organization at which he or she works, the street address, city, state or province, and postal code. That's a lot of stuff but we're still not done. We next put in a salutation: We say "Dear Mary," if we know the recipient well; "Dear Ms. Bonner," if we don't or if we simply want to maintain a level of formality in the correspondence. Occasionally in business letters we might write something like "RE: Recent activity in your investment portfolio" to give the recipient an idea what the letter is about. However, that's pretty rare. Instead, we usually start the body of the letter right after the salutation and make whatever points we wish to make. At the end of the letter, we use a complimentary close ("Sincerely," for example, or "Very truly yours,"), we sign the letter in ink, with our full name and (usually) job title printed beneath our signature.

What about formatting e-mails? At this point, it's much less well defined. For example, there's no real equivalent to the inside address we use in a letter. You just type in the recipient's e-mail address (or select it from a drop list) and let it go at that. However, every e-mail has a subject line where we can identify what we're writing about, and we really need to use it. Sending an e-mail with a blank subject line is foolish unless you want to run the risk of having your message deleted as spam. And using a generic subject line, such as "Update," isn't much better than doing nothing.

Inside the body of the e-mail, people are uncertain what to do in terms of a salutation. Do we say "Dear Mike"? Do we just say "Mike—"? A lot of people like to say something like "Hi, Mike—." Some people don't say anything at all. They just start their message. That's pretty common in e-mails that are sent to a large number of recipients. Otherwise, what do you say? "Hey, everybody—"? At the end of the e-mail there's a similar lack of consistency. Some people end with a variation of the complimentary close, something like "Regards," or "Best wishes," but a lot of people don't use anything at all. Most people type their name at the end of their e-mails, but even that's not universal. I guess some of them figure that you already know who the message is from based on the e-mail address of the sender. Of course, that's not a very good assumption if your e-mail moniker is something like Chihuahuaboy86@hotmail.com. Your e-mail system may enable you to put a signature at the end of every e-mail, and even to vary the signature depending on whether your message is one you have created or one where you're replying to somebody else. The signature can contain pretty much anything you want, including graphics, but it's most useful in a business setting if you include your name, title, company or organization, and your phone numbers. It's a very good idea to provide this information in your e-mails. It looks professional, and it makes it easier for your recipients to recognize you and follow up with you by phone if that's necessary.

I've covered the differences between e-mail and letters at some length because I wanted to emphasize that they are quite different forms of communication. E-Mails aren't simply business letters written in a digitized environment.

The Core Principles of the Language of Success

Why is some writing easy to read and understand? Why does some writing utterly fail? And, most mysterious of all, why is that a given piece of writing is quite clear to you while I can't make any sense of it?

There are five qualities that characterize effective, successful writing. If your e-mails, letters, reports, and proposals consistently embody these characteristics, you will communicate successfully. Successful writing must be:

a. Clear
b. Concise
c. Correct
d. Suited to its audience
e. Suited to its purpose

Improving your writing in just one of these areas will make it more successful. Improving it in all five will make it stand out. The first three characteristics are probably no surprise to you. We know from our own experience as readers that we value writing that's clear and concise. In fact, when I ask groups with whom I am working to list the qualities of successful writing, they almost always start with "clear," "concise," "gets to the point," "no mistakes," "easy to read," and similar comments. The last two characteristics may not be quite as obvious, but getting those two right is critical to your success. In fact, understanding *why* you're writing—the purpose—and to *whom* you are writing—your audience—enables you to make correct decisions during the process of composition. Figure 3.2 illustrates the point.

Knowing your audience, particularly their level of understanding and their basic personality, will make it easy for you to choose the right words and details for your message, to construct readable sentences, and to include examples that make your point vivid. Knowing why you're writing, what your message is supposed to accomplish, will give you the insight you need to select the right structural pattern for the document as a whole and to use effective paragraphs to make your points easier to understand.

I'll take a detailed look at all five of these principles in the following pages, showing you how to write clearly and concisely, discussing some elements of correctness, and going into detail on modifying the message to match the audience and modifying the structure to match your purpose. Then, in Chapter 4, I'll apply the

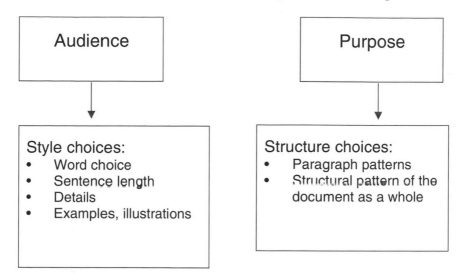

Figure 3.2   Audience and purpose: How they determine your writing choices.

principles to specific kinds of documents. In my opinion, mastering the five principles in this section will be far more important to your long-term success as a writer than looking at a bunch of examples. It's the difference between giving somebody a fish and teaching him how to fish. The next section contains a bunch of fish, but in this section I'll show you how to bait the hook and cast your line into the choicest spots of the stream.

Clarity

Clarity is the first rule of effective communication. If someone has to read what you wrote more than once to understand it, you messed up. No exceptions. Our goal should be to write so clearly that the reader gets it the first time.

We've all had the experience of reading something important, of trying to concentrate, only to go back halfway through the paragraph or the page and start reading it again. We didn't go back because we were enjoying the process so much we wanted to savor the experience once more before the moment was lost. No, we went back because we lost the thread of meaning. In these situations, our brain goes blue screen—we're blank, lost, utterly without a clue. So we go back and start reading again, but this time we tiptoe through the minefield of text that brought us down the first time, rearranging it, stretching it, editing it, trying to figure out what the author intended. If you've read a contract or a technical manual or an academic essay, you've had this experience.

But what does it take to live by this "First Time Right" rule? How do we do it? Nobody's going to argue with advice to "Be clear!" But nobody's going to find that advice very helpful, either. The question is *How?*

Okay. Fair enough. Here goes my attempt to explain how to be clear.

Writing that's easy to read and easy to understand—the essence of readability—is a function of word choice and syntax. When we read, our brain has to do a number of things simultaneously. Some of them are so easy for us, thanks to constant repetition, that they are nearly automatic. For example, we no longer have to look at each letter and try to recall what sound it stands for, laboriously stringing sounds together like a first grader, listening for something that's similar to a word we know from speech. Usually within the first few years of learning to read, we get beyond that. But at the word level, we still need to dredge up all the potential meanings for each word unit. This bit of analysis occurs in an instant, each word blossoming in its richness of meaning. We're not usually conscious of this process, because it happens at lightning speed. But if we can't pinpoint the meaning of each word, we can't get the meaning of the whole.

At the same time, our brain is decoding the syntax—the structure of the sentence. We recognize which words are nouns,

> *To Write Clearly*
>
> 1. Keep your sentences short.
> 2. Use words of one and two syllables most of the time.
> 3. Write mainly in active voice.
> 4. Avoid starting your sentence with long, dependent clauses up front.
> 5. Start each paragraph with the key idea in a topic sentence.

which are verbs, which are adjectives. We decode all the parts of speech, and we grasp how they relate to each other. This sequential analysis causes us to eliminate certain meanings from the preceding words. Rather quickly, the two elements of reading—(1) recognizing the way words are sequenced and the relationships among them and (2) calling up all the potential meanings we know and then narrowing them down to a relevant few—produce meaning.

When does this process break down? It breaks down when we overload the system. If the words are so obscure or difficult or simply contain too many letters, they put our brain under pressure to surface meanings that work. And if the sentence is too long or too complicated, we may find that we can't navigate our way through it. We can't figure out which words relate to which other words in it. As a result, we lose track of the meaning and end up confused. Our brain incurs a "general protection fault" and crashes.

But there is a solution. Simplify! Simplify the words and shorten the sentences. The impact on clarity is dramatic.

Standardized measures of readability use the two key factors I mentioned—word choice and sentence length—to determine how readable a piece of writing is. Editors of materials aimed at children, for example, use formulas to determine whether a particular piece of writing is appropriate for the grade level where it will be used. You can use similar indices to determine whether your writing is clear enough for educated adults.

The easiest way to do this, if you use Microsoft Word, is to click on Tools: Options and then click on the tab labeled "Grammar & Spelling." Near the bottom of the tab are two check boxes, "Check grammar with spelling" and "Show readability statistics." Put a check mark in both boxes, and the computer will now automatically calculate how readable your writing is. After completing a spelling and grammar check, the program will show you a summary of your key readability statistics. The one you should look at first is the one at the bottom. It's called the "Flesch-Kincaid Grade Level," and you want it to be below 12. In fact, if it's 10 or less you'll be doing very well.

Here are the readability statistics for the previous paragraph:

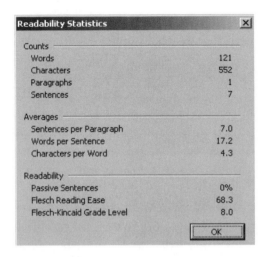

As you can see, the Flesch-Kincaid Grade Level for that paragraph is pretty good—the computer tells us it's at 8, which is way below the danger line of 12. (Don't get hung up on the notion of grade level. We're not talking about how much education you reader has. We're just talking about how complex the language is. A grade level of 8 to 10 is about what you'll find in front page articles in the *Wall Street Journal* or *The New York Times,* and those are obviously intended for intelligent adults.)

The next most important piece of information in that chart is the average number of words per sentence. You want to write with an average sentence length of around 15 to 17 words per sentence. The chart shows us that the paragraph in question is about at that level, which is good. As we said earlier, when the sentences are too long, the reader is more likely to lose the thread of thought and have to go back to read it again. And that's taboo.

Finally, note the percentage of passive voice sentences: 0%. That's also good. As a guideline, you want to keep the percentage of passive voice to 10% or less. A higher percentage than that will slow down readability.

If you don't have access to your word processor, you can use Robert Gunning's Fog Index, one of the first of the readability formulas and one of the simplest. In fact, you can do the calculations in your head. To figure out the Fog Index, start with a chunk of text that's about a hundred words long. Count how many sentences there are in your sample, and divide the number of sentences into the total number of words. That will give you the average sentence length. As I mentioned, anything around 15 to 17 words is a good average sentence length for adult readers. Anything above 20 is bordering on unreadable, and anything above 30 is a disaster. Let's say in our 100-word sample, we have four sentences. That means the average sentence length is 25. (And that means they're too long!)

The next step in Gunning's formula is to count how many big words your chunk of text contains. A big word, by definition, is any word that has three syllables or more. You need to use your judgment here, since some two-syllable verbs ("transport") acquire a third syllable with a verb ending—"transported" or "transporting," for example. On the other hand, a bit of jargon or an acronym might count even though it's very short. What's a good average percentage for big words? Ten percent is fine. Any higher than 15 percent is going to be a problem. Now let's say in our hypothetical sample we count 12 words that have three syllables or more. That's a bit high, but not terrible.

The final step in calculating the Fog Index is to add the two numbers together and multiply the sum by .4. So in our case, we would add the average sentence length of 25 to the number of big words, 12, getting 37. We multiply 37 by .4 and the answer is 14.8. That's our grade level equivalent. You already know that 12 is the danger line and that 10 is more desirable than 12. So a grade level score of 14.8 is much too high. You should aim for a score of 10 or lower, perhaps quite a bit lower depending on your individual circumstances. Keeping the score low doesn't mean you think your readers are stupid. Rather, it's a recognition that they may be extremely busy or that they may be completely unfamiliar with your topic. My theory is that our brains can apply only a finite amount of energy to processing information at one time. Part of that energy is allocated to figuring out what the words mean as we read. Another part of that energy is allocated to decoding the sentences. Whatever is left after those two jobs are finished is allocated to understanding the meaning. If we are using such complex language that there's nothing left, the reader will never get the meaning.

All right, let's take a look at a sample piece of writing. This is an excerpt from a long e-mail written to a client:

Based on your strategic plan and priorities as explained to us in a series of management meetings over the past six weeks and in numerous memos, phone calls, and a draft proposal which you have reviewed, a partnership with us will provide you with the tools and resources to develop and implement strategies to improve your financial and operational performance with group purchasing, supply chain management, warehousing, transportation cycle management, management reporting and information, and education. Our national and regional suite of supply chain and transportation options is the most direct and immediate route to enhanced operational performance by reducing costs up to 60 to 65 percent. Through our unique mix of tools for designing and managing the supply chain, we can collaborate toward the objective of a total spend management by establishing a comprehensive supply chain strategy, analyzing the opportunities, automating key processes, and using outsourcing and system redundancy to reduce supply chain costs by 10 percent or more.

Is that clear to you? I'll confess that I find it hard to read. There's nothing particularly complicated about the content. It doesn't even have a lot of jargon. It's 131 words long and consists of only three sentences, giving us an average sentence length of 43+! No wonder it feels like we're slogging through a swamp. And when you add up the number of three-syllable words—32 of them by my count—you can see that the writer has given us a tough row of verbiage to hoe. In fact, the Fog Index on this passage is a depressing 30!

Beyond these problems, the whole passage seems redundant and confusing. It repeats the words "operational," "supply chain," "transportation," "tools," and "resources" a number of times until we feel like we're swirling around in circles. Plus, I find it confusing to be told that we can reduce costs "up to 60 to 65 percent," only to be told a few words later that we can "reduce supply chain costs by 10 percent or more." Which is it?

So how can we fix all of this? It's not easy, because in a couple of spots we can't be sure what the writer meant to say. But if we make some reasonable guesses, we get something like this:

You have indicated that improving operational performance in your transportation system is a strategic priority for your firm. Our goal is to help you achieve that goal by providing you with specialized tools and resources. Some of these tools will cut costs by giving you access to group purchasing, improving your supply chain management, and enabling you to coordinate your warehousing and transportation more efficiently. We will also provide other tools and resources that will make it easier for you to keep track of your operations by improving your reporting and information systems. What is the impact of the tools and resources we provide? Many of our clients have reduced costs as much as 60 to 65 percent.

The process is simple and direct. We will collaborate with you in a phased approach that identifies your potential savings. First, we will establish a comprehensive supply chain strategy. Then we will analyze the opportunities in your business. Next, we will automate your key processes. Finally, we will help you identify opportunities to outsource or eliminate system redundancies to drive out costs.

That's better, isn't it? What have we done to improve it?

First, we broke it into two separate paragraphs, one focusing on the how the operations will be improved and the other focusing on the steps to make that happen. Shorter paragraphs are easier to digest. An easy rule to remember here is that each paragraph should have its own independent topic. If you're in doubt, you're better off breaking the paragraph up and using a transition sentence to explain what the next paragraph will be about.

Second, we broke up the three long sentences into twelve short ones. The average sentence length is now below 15 words, and the readability index is down to 10.

Third, we got rid of the long dependent clause at the start of the paragraph ("Based on your strategic plan . . . blah, blah, blah . . . which you have reviewed"). A dependent clause up front is tough because it requires our readers to keep a big chunk of content in suspension until they read on and find out what it's modifying or what it's related to. There's nothing wrong with that kind of construction grammatically. But it makes the reading process harder, and that means our writing will not seem clear.

Fourth, we used stronger subject/verb constructions. In the first sentence of the original version, the main subject/verb relationship is " . . . a partnership . . . will provide . . . ." In the second sentence, the subject and verb are "suite" and "is" respectively. Any time "is" is the main verb in your sentence, particularly a long sentence, there's a good chance the sentence will sound weak or unfocused. In the revision, the subjects/verbs are "you/have indicated," "goal/is," "tools/will cut," "we/will provide," "impact/is [inverted for the question]," and "Many/have reduced." These are a little better, but the biggest improvement comes from the fact each verb carries less syntactic weight—the sentences that hang from them are much shorter and much more comprehensible.

Here's another example:

> We have structured our team to maximize our capability to ensure that we can be responsive to both current and future customer needs and to ensure that we have redundant, yet complementary, capabilities and ample resources to respond to your increasing and evolving requirements. Our key management features include a streamlined, integrated teaming partnership (contractor and customer); successful execution of large, worldwide labor hour contracts using the most accepted project management methodologies; proven Web-based management tools providing continuous performance visibility (team and customer); a management infrastructure with personnel backgrounds deeply rooted within the requisite technical disciplines, including a premier senior advisory committee; and a proactive, empowered workforce; all fully aligned with your overarching mission and strategy.

So how did that "First time right" rule work out for you with this one? Did you lose your train of thought? Did you skip right through the example after a few lines? I wouldn't be surprised if you bailed out on this pretty quickly, because it's very hard to follow.

Obviously, the sentences are too long here. The entire paragraph consists of just two sentences and a total of 116 words, giving us an average sentence length of 58 words. (That's about four times longer than what we're looking for.) In addition, it's written using lots of abstractions in the first sentence ("maximize," "capability," "ensure," "responsive," "resources," "evolving," "requirements") and lots of dependent clauses in the second. Also, saying that our team has "redundant . . . capabilities" probably sends the wrong message. Let's try fixing it:

We have assembled a team that has all the skills necessary to meet your current needs and those that are likely to arise in the future. The team includes experts with overlapping and complementary skills, so we can always respond quickly to your needs. And we have provided them with the resources they need, recognizing that your work environment is likely to become more complex and demanding.

The key features of our management approach include:

Effective project methods and tools—
- a streamlined, integrated teaming partnership (for both you and us)
- a body of knowledge based on successfully executing large, worldwide labor hour contracts
- use of the most accepted project management methodologies
- proven Web-based management tools that will give both of us continuous performance visibility

The right team—
- a management team that includes people with backgrounds deeply rooted in the right technologies
- a senior advisory committee with outstanding experience
- a proactive, empowered workforce
- alignment of our work with your overarching mission and strategy

---

This is easier to understand, although far from perfect. The number of sentences has gone from two to twelve, if we count each bullet point as a separate "sentence"—which is what the brain does when it encounters them. (Or, more accurately, it treats them as discrete syntactic units.) The average sentence length is now a little under 14. We've grouped the points that support our ability to do a good job into two categories, thus avoiding giving the reader a longish list of bullet points. But it still contains a lot of buzz words ("proactive," "empowered," "alignment," "integrated," and so on). We'd have to speak to the author to find out exactly what he or she was trying to say, but in any event we would want to eliminate these manifestations of Guff.

I think we're at a point where we can summarize our thoughts about clarity. By definition, clear writing is writing that has to be read only once to be understood. To achieve that kind of clarity:

- We should keep the average sentence length to something reasonable—around 15 words or so.
- We should avoid using big, unfamiliar words, technical jargon, and acronyms.
- We should organize paragraphs coherently, by using a general topic sentence at the outset and then supporting the point made in the topic sentence with details in the sentences that follow.
- And we should avoid writing sentences with lots of embedded clauses, particularly long dependent clauses at the start.

Conciseness

Wordiness is one of the most common complaints that I hear from business people about the writing they have to read. Wordy writing seems to just go on and on and never gets to a point. You feel like you're wasting your time, because . . . well, you are. The writer hasn't said anything that couldn't have been said in half the words.

For example, consider this little gem from an email setting up a meeting:

For this program, it is proposed that the kick-off meeting be one day in length with the first half of the day consisting of the following activities:

- Greetings, introductions, and opportunity to get acquainted
- Overview of the session
- Review of the market situation and competitive environment
- Summary of customer feedback from the surveys completed last quarter

---

Sound familiar? This is pretty typical of how people write when they're trying to sound impressive or when they don't have a clue what they're going to say until they're halfway through their message. It's not impressive; it's just annoying. And it's a safe bet you'll get to your point quicker if you know what it is before you start writing. Then say it in as few words as possible. Before you hit *send*, take the time to jot down your thoughts. Then take the time to edit your work before sending it out. Look for ways to cut unnecessary words. Replace long clauses with a phrase, a phrase with a word. If you just send out stream-of-consciousness memos like the one above, you will inevitably create a bad impression, and in the future people will start skimming your messages or even skipping them completely.

As your read the example, you probably spotted ways to cut it way, way down. Maybe you were envisioning something like this:

I recommend a one-day kick-off meeting with the first half covering:

* Introductions
* Session overview
* The market and competition
* Summary of last quarter's customer surveys

We cut the total words from 60 to 28 and made the message clearer in the process. The example was wordier than most writing, but the fact is we can often squeeze a third of the total words out of our writing without losing the message.

Using phrases where a single word would do will make your writing wordy and annoying. So will converting perfectly healthy verbs into nouns. Here are some examples of both mistakes:

advance plan	plan
study in depth	study
consensus of opinion	consensus
in the majority of instances	usually
for the purpose of	for
at this time	now

with regard to	regarding
in order to	to
take action	act
have a discussion	discuss
hold a meeting	meet

Each of these examples illustrates a type of mistake that creates wordiness. The first, "advance plan," illustrates the use of an unnecessary qualifier. What other kind of plan would we create? A retroactive plan? Similar errors include "true facts," "past experience," "sudden crisis," and "basic fundamentals."

The second, "study in depth," is an example of using an unnecessary determiner—in this case, "in depth." The meaning of "study" makes it unlikely we would do it "superficially," so the phrase "in depth" is unnecessary. A phrase frequently used in high-tech circles to describe networks and systems, "highly available," also contains an unnecessary qualification. We wouldn't be interested in a network that was "occasionally available." The concept of availability argues against that.

The third example illustrates repetitious redundancy. That was a joke, but also an accurate description of the problem. "Consensus" means the majority opinion of a group, so the phrase "consensus of opinion" is painfully redundant. It's similar to saying "green in color," or the expression in our sample e-mail about the meeting, above, which said the kick-off meeting would be "one day in length . . . " What else would it be? One day in height? Another popular one is to write "7 A.M. in the morning." But A.M. already refers to the morning. Otherwise it would be P.M., right?

Writing "in the majority of instances" rather than "usually" or "normally" might be a good idea if you're paid by the word. The same is true of "for the purpose of . . . " Otherwise, forget it. Likewise, don't say "the reason why is because. . . ." Instead, simply say "because" and be done with it.[4]

The last three examples, "take action," "have a discussion," and "hold a meeting," are instances of what grammarians call

---

[4]Kim Blank, an English professor at the University of Victoria has posted a comprehensive list of expressions to cut or compress at http://web.uvic.ca/~gkblank/wordiness.html. You can find other useful Web resources by entering "wordiness" in Google.

nominalization. All that means is that words that usually function as verbs have been converted into nouns. Weaker, less specific verbs have been attached to them. Compare these instances and tell me which is more concise and emphatic:

We decided to take action now.	We decided to act now.
We will have a discussion about the parking problems affecting the visitor's lot.	We will discuss the parking problems affecting the visitor's lot.
You may need to hold a meeting just to review the grant applications.	You may need to meet just to review the grant applications.
Our software stack proved to provide more functionality.	Our software stack provided more functionality.
We achieved elimination of the problem through the addition of a flow meter at the input valve.	We eliminated the problem by adding a flow meter at the input valve.
Our notification of intention to provide refunds was sent to our customers yesterday.	We notified customers yesterday that we intend to provide refunds.

I've often wondered why writers convert verbs into nouns. Why do they write:

The function of the interface is the improvement of user productivity.

Customers displayed a preference for the mint-flavored over the cherry-flavored cough syrups.

We took a measurement of the decibel levels a quarter mile from the main runway.

Instead of:

The interface improves user productivity.

Customers preferred the mint-flavored over the cherry-flavored cough syrups.

We measured decibel levels a quarter mile from the main runway.

I don't get it. Maybe using nominalizations is a misguided attempt at elegance. Maybe the writer thinks it sounds more intellectual or sophisticated to write that way. Maybe it's just sloppy thinking. Regardless, train your ear to hear these constructions so you can eliminate them from your writing.

A more fundamental problem arises when the writer sends us a message we didn't need to see in the first place. When that happens, it's pretty clear that *all* of the words can be cut with no loss. A friend of mine, Hank, sent me an example of an e-mail he found hilarious that illustrates the problem of pointless messages. A young marketing assistant, whom we will call "Lisa," had sent his design team more than twenty separate e-mails filled with lots of scattered details affecting a couple of different projects. He finally told Lisa to stop sending so many messages. Instead, consolidate all of the details into one complete message on what needed to be done by the designers. Lisa apparently didn't get the point, because her next e-mail was a useless message explaining what she was planning to send in the future in two separate e-mails:

> To: Hank
> Subject: 2 emails that are coming
>
> Hank,
>
> I am sending you 2 separate emails for our projects.
>
> The first email will consist of: The three one-sheets (Xavier and YMCA) and the Organic Foods one-sheet The second email: Wilton one-sheet and Vane & Roberts one sheet.
>
> I will send the first one first and the second one will come later.
>
> Thanks,
>
> Lisa

Based on the last sentence of her message, Lisa seems to have a remarkable gift for stating the obvious. However, she's not quite as gifted in communicating anything else. Thanks to her bizarre punctuation and capitalization, the previous sentence, which details what the two future e-mails will contain, is extremely hard to follow. Lisa's message proves that before you can get to the point you need to have a point.

Before we drop the topic of conciseness, it's fair to ask: Can we have too much of a good thing? Can we cut the words down so much we actually damage clarity?

> *Words to Write By . . .*
>
> Before you can get to the point, you need to have a point.

Yes, we can. It happens when we eliminate some of the functional words that show how a sentence is glued together. Perhaps an analogy will help explain what I mean. Not long ago I went to one of the Web-based mapping systems to get driving directions from an airport to the hotel where I was booked. The system gave me some options: avoiding highways, avoiding toll roads, taking the shortest distance, or taking the quickest route. I must have made some kind of odd choice among those combinations, because I ended up with a map that laid out what was probably the shortest route to follow in terms of total miles but which got me stuck in a five-way intersection at rush hour. Although the total miles were less, my actual travel time was much longer. This is similar to what happens when we compress our writing down to the point that it becomes difficult to read.

Here's an example, which came from a corporate announcement:

> The earth resources satellite field station installation maintenance repair manual has been published.

That sentence contains only thirteen words, yet it's very hard to understand, because it uses nine nouns in a row. As a result, our beleaguered brains search desperately for some clues as to how those nouns function in the sentence. Only one of them is actually a noun—"manual." All the rest are adjectives. If we rearrange the sentence to let some of the nouns function as nouns, we end up using a few more words but the sentence seems more concise:

> The manual for installing, maintaining, and repairing the field station for the earth resources satellite has been published.

Now we've used eighteen words to express the same basic message. But isn't it easier to understand? Because the syntax—the way the sentence is put together and how the words relate to each other— is easier to understand, the sentence is now easier to decode.

This kind of construction, which I call a *noun cluster*, is very common in technical writing. You'll see writing like this all the time:

> One advantage that we offer is specialized technology solutions integration services.

This would be clearer—and, again, would seem more concise— if it were written:

> One advantage we offer is specialized services to integrate technology solutions.

Being clear is more important than being concise. You've made a bad bargain if you trade the clarity of your message for saying it in fewer words. Our goal, though, should be to write messages that maximize both qualities. A clear message will have more impact and will be more memorable, if it's also a concise message. Combine them in a single piece of writing and the reader will understand.

Correctness

Because we must control writing more carefully than speech to make sure we communicate effectively, we must be accurate and precise in our writing. Grammar errors that we ignore in spoken English become glaring flaws in writing. Slang that we tolerate in speech sounds obnoxious or silly when written.

We need to write accurately and precisely. That means having our facts straight, getting the details right, using words correctly, and minimizing errors in grammar, spelling, and punctuation. I'm not going to give you any advice regarding the first two. If you can't get the facts straight or the details right, you have bigger problems than a slim book on business writing can fix.

But we should take a minute to consider the importance of being accurate and precise in our word choice, usage, grammar, spelling, and punctuation. Mistakes in those areas undercut our credibility, imply that we don't respect the audience enough to proofread, and suggest an inability to manage simple tasks professionally. Misspellings, grammar mistakes, punctuation blunders: All of them add up line by line to become a huge distraction, a kind of background noise that drowns out the actual message.

Mark Twain pointed out that spelling has little correlation to the significance or importance of a message. "I'd rather be locked in a train car on a long journey with somebody who can think well rather than somebody who can spell well," he said. Twain's principle is correct: An e-mail or report that has zero spelling mistakes might still have zero useful content. But a document that's riddled with misspelled words won't be taken seriously. Especially in this era of automatic spelling checkers, there's no excuse for putting out a document containing a lot of errors.

The explosive growth of text messaging has also led to an increase in the use of odd, sometimes creative, often mystifying spelling. Some of it looks like the sort of thing we see on personalized license plates—"That's gr8!"—and some of it seems to be freeze dried, with all the "unnecessary" letters squeezed out—"Cld y mt @ 3?" Writing this way saves wear and tear on your thumbs when you're sending instant messages, and perhaps reduces the likelihood of accidents for those people who insist on texting while driving their car. But it has no place in business e-mails, letters, or reports. For people who write a lot of instant messages, there's a risk that this kind of shorthand will slip into standard writing. In some environments, there is also a risk that these messages will be sent or forwarded to a boss, whether accidentally or by a mischievous coworker.

Some misspellings come from mistaking one word for another. The confusion between "its" and "it's" is perhaps the most common. I've noticed this particular mistake in books, magazines, billboards, even the credits of movies: "The producers would like to thank the citizens of Lower Skankway for their hospitality and the Skankway police department for it's cooperation." *And our grade school for "it's" education of us?*

If you didn't turn on your spelling and grammar checker earlier when I pointed out that it will also calculate readability for you, do it now. Use the grammar checker until you are positive that you can comfortably and reliably handle the fundamentals of grammar. Never turn off your spell checker, neither on your e-mail system nor your word processor. Add words to the spell checker's dictionary if a particular proper name or other word keeps tripping it up. But never turn it off. It's your servant. Make it work for you.

> **Words to Write By . . .**
>
> The main reason to follow the rules of standard English is to minimize background noise that could drown out your message.

Bear in mind, however, that there are some errors the computer usually won't catch. These mistakes arise from confusing one word with another one that looks and sounds similar. English is filled with odd, confusing pairs. Why do we say "their," "they're," and "there" the same way when they mean totally different things? What's the difference between "insure," "ensure," and "assure"? Here are some words that are frequently misused. Becoming familiar with their correct usage will eliminate a lot of errors from your emails, letters, and other business documents.

affect / effect

Effect is usually a noun that means "a result," "an impact," or "a consequence": "Judge Green's decision had an effect on the future of telecommunications in the United States." *Affect* is usually a verb that means "to influence" or "to cause": "The generator's failure affected our ability to continue emergency operations." This pair of words is particularly confusing because *effect* is sometimes used as a verb to mean "to bring about," "to cause to happen," or "to execute." This usage is primarily limited to lawyers, who should never be trusted when it comes to clear writing (or so says my son, Christopher, who is one): "The nondisclosure clause effected restrictions on what information we could share with our subcontractors." Likewise, *affect* can be used as a noun, usually by psychologists or psychiatrists, to describe someone's emotional tone: "Although his depression has lifted, he still displays a blunted affect." Unless you're a licensed attorney or psychiatrist, forget about these usages and stick to the most common meanings: *effect* is a noun; *affect* is a verb.

alternately / alternatively

Alternately means "one after the other": "We alternately presented our sales figures and our projections for the coming month for each of the product lines." *Alternatively* means "on the other hand;" or "one or the other": "You can choose a support package for regular business hours or, alternatively, you can get full coverage 24 hours a day, seven days a week."

anxious / eager

Are you *anxious* to do business with us? Or are you *eager*? If you're *anxious*, perhaps you'd like to explain why so that we can feel anxious too. *Anxious* suggests that you are "nervous" or "worried," in a state of anxiety or mental distress, so don't use it as a synonym for *eager*.

beside / besides

Beside means "next to": "Please sit beside me at the conference." *Besides* means "in addition to" or "also." "Besides your presentation at the start of the meeting, we will also have a short training session on the new phone system."

bimonthly / semimonthly [also, biannual / semiannual]

Bimonthly means every two months; *semimonthly* means twice a month. "At our office we have a bimonthly office party." That would mean you have six parties a year. If you say, "We have semimonthly parties in our office," you're having twenty-four of them a year. Sounds like four times more fun to me. Let's be honest here: Most of us get confused on this one, so isn't it safer just to say "twice a month"? Our readers will secretly thank us.

capital / capitol

The money or other assets a person has acquired is his or her *capital*. The same word describes the money a firm invests in equipment or facilities: "These capital investments will pay off over the long term." Here's where it gets tricky: The city where the state government is located is also called the *capital*, which can be confusing because the building where Congress or the state legislature holds its proceedings is called the *capitol*. By the way, the word *capital* is also used to describe the kind of letter we use to start a sentence.

cite / site / sight

Cite means to quote as an authority or example: "I cited several comments from customers verbatim in our marketing brochure." It also means to receive official recognition as a form of commendation ("cited for years of service") or, confusingly, as a legal sanction ("cited for violations of standard accounting practices"). *Site* means "location": "You indicated that you would like our help in selecting the most promising sites for ten additional retail outlets." "The Internet contains innumerable Web sites." *Sight* is a noun describing one of the five senses: "The goals we set at the start of the year are now within sight." *Sight* has other meanings ("a gun sight"; "a sight designed to please"), but they're related to our ability to see.

complement / compliment

Complement means to complete or make whole: "Our installation services complement our product sales." *Compliment* means praise or flattery: "We must compliment you for the efficient way you handled our sudden request for 500 additional guests at the banquet."

comprise / compose

This pair is really tricky. If you check a good dictionary, it'll probably tell you that the whole *comprises* the parts, and the parts *compose* the whole. Technically, you would say "The review panel comprises five experts in oncology," or "Five experts in oncology compose the review panel." However, *comprise* is often used in passive voice constructions: "The PacWest sales region is comprised of California, Oregon, Washington, Nevada, and Arizona." You're better off simply saying: "The board is made up of twelve outside and five inside members."

concurrent / consecutive

Concurrent means "simultaneous" or "happening at the same time as something else": "The concurrent release of new products in five core markets overwhelmed our telemarketing operation." *Consecutive* means "one after the other": "Next year we will stage new product releases, putting them out in consecutive quarters rather than all at once."

council / councilor / counsel / counselor

A *council* is an assembly or group called together for discussion or deliberation, so a *councilor* is a member of one. A *counselor* is somebody who gives *counsel*, which is another word for "advice" or "guidance."

discreet / discrete

Discreet means keeping things quiet, or behaving in a "prudent," "circumspect," or "modest" manner: "The HR department handled the sexual harassment suit discreetly." *Discrete* means "separate" or "individual": "To operate as a true profit center, our business unit needs a discrete budget for sales and marketing."

data is / data are

Data is should be used unless you are referring to disparate kinds of data. I know, I know. Some of you studied Latin or at least served as altar boys or girls. I can see your hands waving in the air, trying to get my attention. "Teacher, teacher, *data* is plural in Latin! *Datum* is the singular. "Okay, you're right, so if you write any e-mails to the Pope, make sure you use it that way. However, for all of your correspondents and colleagues for whom English is the language of choice, you need to remember that *data* is a collective noun, which is a grammar term applied to nouns that name a collection of things: *team, jury, committee, class, regiment,* and so on. Collective nouns take a singular verb when they refer to the group as a whole: "The data is stored at our data center in Milwaukee." When a collective noun refers to components or individuals within the group, it takes a plural verb: "The accounting, sales, and engineering data are being backed up."

disinterested / uninterested

Disinterested means "neutral," "unbiased," or "impartial": "We expected the judge to be disinterested, but learned to our chagrin that he had a conflict of interest." *Uninterested* means "not interested," "bored," or "indifferent": "The applicant seemed uninterested in whether we hired him."

e.g. / i.e.

The acronym *e.g.* means "for example," and each letter should be followed by a period. It comes from a Latin expression, *exempli gratia.* You use *e.g.* whenever you could also use *for example:* "Her resume listed some interesting hobbies—e.g., slam poetry festivals, downhill ski racing, and speed chess." The abbreviation *i.e.* means "that is" (from the Latin expression *id est):* "Overall quality improvements (i.e., fewer rejected parts and fewer defects noted at final inspection) increased net profitability last quarter." By the way, both of these acronyms should always be followed by commas, as I did in the preceding examples.

farther / further

Farther relates to distance—going to or being located at a *farther* point. "How much farther will our delivery trucks need to go with the new route structures?" *Further* means "to or at a greater extent or degree": "When the clinical trials are further along, we'll assess the efficacy of both treatment regimens." *Further* can also mean "in addition" or "moreover." Sometimes that usage becomes *furthermore*: "The chief financial officer testified that he had no further knowledge of the options that were granted to the CEO. Furthermore, he said the options were, in his opinion, excessive."

flammable / inflammable

This has to be most useless pair of confusing words in the language, because they mean the exact same thing: Don't light that match! But *inflammable* looks like it should mean the opposite, since the prefix *in-* often means negation, as in "insincere," "incomplete," and so on. I vote to abolish the word "inflammable," especially on the back of fuel trucks. Who's with me on this?

foreword / forward

A *foreword* is the introductory note or preface that appears at the front of a book or major report: "In the foreword we listed our key evaluation criteria, but many of the readers missed them." *Forward* means toward the front: "My boss kept creeping forward during my presentation, which I found very disconcerting." *Forward* is also used to describe what we do to e-mailed jokes, chain letters, pictures of cute baby animals, and stuff like that. Oh, wait. That word is *delete.*

insure / ensure / assure

These words have related meanings. They all mean to make something secure or certain. Firms on the east coast of the United States tend to call themselves "life assurance" companies, but it's far more common to refer to life (or health, fire, casualty, car, etc.) *insurance* elsewhere in the country. The differences among these words are pretty subtle. Basically, *insure* implies a binding commitment: "The investment firm required us to insure our key executives' lives." *Ensure* has the connotation of making serious effort: "We planned our move carefully to ensure there would be no down time for our customers." *Assure* implies a personal commitment and the sense of putting someone's worries to rest: "Let me assure you that every effort will be made to locate the missing funds."

its / it's [also, your / you're; whose / who's ; theirs / there's]

People often confuse possessive pronouns, which do not require an apostrophe, with contractions, which do require one. Possessive pronouns show ownership when they are used alone, they end with an "s" or the "s" sound: *yours, his, hers, ours, theirs, whose.* (The exception is the pronoun *mine.*) We would ask or write, "Is this book yours?" And someone might answer, "No, it's hers." (When the pronoun modifies a noun, we drop the "s" sound": *your book, her computer, our presentation.*) We don't make many mistakes with *hers, his,* or *ours,* because there aren't any other words that sound the same. But *its, your,* and *whose* create problems. A simple rule: If you're using a pronoun and you're forming a contraction between that pronoun and a verb, you need an apostrophe. Thus, *it's, you're,* and *who's* mean *it is, you are,* and *who is,* respectively. Try saying the words separately in the sentence. Does it make sense? If so, it's a contraction (or, it is a contraction, to apply my own principle) and you need an apostrophe.

> *Words to Write By . . .*
>
> Contractions always require an apostrophe.

lead / led / lead

Lead, pronounced with a long *e* sound to rhyme with "speed," is a verb, meaning to show the way (among other meanings). The past tense of that verb is *led. Lead,* pronounced with a short *e* sound to rhyme with "red," is a dense, heavy metal.

loose / lose

Loose describes the way your pants fit if you've been on a diet. *Lose* is the opposite of *win* or of *find*. For some reason, people get these two words confused all the time, which is odd since they don't even sound the same.

penultimate

Penultimate sounds like it should be "the very last" thing, but it isn't. It means "next to last." Just write "next to last" to avoid confusion, unless you're positive your readers will understand this correctly: "The penultimate step in the project will be completed one week prior to system initiation."

precede / proceed

Precede means to come before something else in time or space: "Budgetary approval must precede any hirings." *Proceed* means to go forward in doing something. "Once you have the budget, you can proceed with hiring the staff you need."

principal / principle

Principal means the main person or thing. The main administrative officer in a high school is the *principal*. Likewise, the senior members of a partnership, such as a law firm, are the *principals*. The main chunk of money you're paying off with your mortgage is the *principal*: "We always pay a little extra against the principal each month along with the interest payment." A *principle* is a rule, a guideline, or an axiom for living. "Some of the principals showed that they have no principles."

serve / service

Do you *serve* your customers or do you *service* them? I suppose it depends on what line of work you're in, but *servicing* somebody has the wrong connotation in most cases: "Every facet of our company is oriented to servicing you, the customer." And if you've ever been serviced with a facet, you know how painful that can be. *Service* is a noun. Using it as a verb creates the wrong impression.

simple / simplistic

Simplistic is sometimes confused with the superlative form of *simple*, which is *simplest*. Actually, *simplistic* is an adjective that means "stupid" or "foolish." Thus, you probably don't want to say, "We worked for several weeks to develop a simplistic project plan for you."

stationary / stationery

Stationary means "fixed" or "unmoving": "Renovations in our office space were hampered by a row of stationary pillars that run down the center aisle, defeating our designer's efforts to create a Caribbean theme." *Stationery* means writing paper: "Our new company stationery jammed the printer."

Suitability for the Audience

Have you ever coached a team of 8-year-old soccer players? Led a troop of Cub Scouts or Brownies? Then you know that you have to speak in a way that gets their attention and is understandable to them. You need to keep your coaching lesson short, relevant, fun, and full of energy. You need to present it using simple, everyday words. Well, most of our adult audiences would appreciate it if we'd do the same for them.

We need to tailor our message so that it is matches our audience's abilities and requirements. That means using words our audience will understand, including details that they will find relevant, and emphasizing points that matter to them. To tailor our language successfully by choosing the right words and including the right amount of detail, we need to know two things:

1. The audience's level of technical or professional expertise—in other words, their level of knowledge
2. The audience's preferences in terms of how they like to interact with other people and with information

These factors matter whether we're writing or presenting in person, but it's a lot easier to figure out if we're not getting our points across when we have the audience right in front of us. If we give them the chance, an audience will stop us to ask questions, seek clarification, or communicate nonverbally that they're not following us. None of those resources are immediately available to our readers. We have to do our best to figure out what the audience needs so we can adjust the message in advance. We don't need to be too precise about it, and as I mentioned earlier we're better off making things too simple and too clear than missing the mark the other way. Let's take a look at each of the factors—level of expertise and personality type—and what we can do to make sure our writing works.

Adjusting for Levels of Expertise   Will Rogers once said, "Everybody's ignorant, just on different stuff." The question you need to answer is just how ignorant your reader is about your subject. If you don't give some conscious thought to the issue, you're likely to write to the one audience you really understand well—yourself. Maybe that will work if you're writing to your exact peers at work. Maybe it'll work if you're writing to your immediate supervisor or your direct subordinates. Otherwise, you need to make an effort to modify the message.

Most of us overestimate our audience's level of understanding, assuming that our readers know more and understand more than they really do. This probably happens because we're writing about concepts, processes, or products that are a core part of our everyday experience. It all seems natural and intuitive to us. But it's not. It's knowledge that we've earned over months or years of education and effort. If we don't get outside our head and into the reader's head, we're likely to write an e-mail, letter, report, or proposal that would be perfect—providing it's going to somebody just like us. Unfortunately, other than a tiny group of colleagues who share our knowledge and experience, nobody will fully understand it because we have left key assumptions unexplained, have left jargon undefined, and thrown around acronyms without explaining them in simple terms.

Sometimes clients ask me if there isn't a danger in making a message too simple. "What if the audience already understands this material? Won't it sound like we're patronizing them? Won't we sound arrogant or condescending?" No, probably not. Arrogance is a tone, not a level of detail. If you communicate in a sincere tone and honestly respect your audience, you're very unlikely to offend anybody. If it happens they know more about our subject than we thought they did and we're covering material they already understand, they'll just skip ahead to the next chunk. No harm done. I can assure you this is definitely not the problem that 99 percent of writers have.

If you're going to make a mistake in estimating the audience's level of understanding, it's much better to aim too low than too high. If you assume they know more than they actually do, they're stuck. Your content will go sailing over their

> *Words to Write By . . .*
>
> It's always better to underestimate the audience's level of understanding than to overestimate it. If in doubt, simplify.

heads and there isn't a thing they can do to make it more intelligible, other than e-mailing you to ask for clarification or calling you on the phone to try to figure out what you're telling them. My philosophy is when in doubt, leave it out. Err on the side of keeping things too simple, not too complex.

On that note, let's keep it simple and define two levels of audience—uninformed and expert—and take a look at the best ways to communicate to each of them.

The uninformed audience.   Labeling people "uninformed" may sound a bit rude, but all we're saying is that they are uninformed in your industry or area of expertise. They're probably very bright and highly educated, just not in the subject that you are writing about. Think of your grandfather, the retired electrician, who can wire a house with his eyes closed but doesn't understand anything about import/export licensing. Think of your neighbor, the bookkeeper for a local car dealership, who doesn't know anything about Web-based marketing. Think of your loving spouse whose eyes can't help glazing over when you start explaining in detail what you did at work. The world contains billions of people who know next to nothing about what you do for a living. Sometimes you have to write to them. When you do, they are your toughest audience.

Although most of your uninformed readers work outside your company, you'll face the same challenge when you have to write to a new hire, to a subject matter expert from a totally unrelated discipline, to your counterpart in another division of your company, or to a general manager whose responsibilities are too broad to allow him or her to keep up with specific technical details.

The uninformed reader has very little patience for details unless they are details that directly concern him or her. These readers are prone to misunderstanding some of the technical content. And they're very likely to skim your document rather than read it completely. As a result, it's a good idea to keep your messages short, business-like, and focused on bottom-line issues. If you're sending an e-mail, you might want to provide the key message at a high level in the e-mail itself and attach any detailed discussion as a separate file that the more expert readers can click on. However, that is not a good idea if the technical details are germane to your main point. For example, suppose you are writing a report about recent lab tests of engine components. Penetrant dye inspection has revealed microscopic crack patterns that suggest something important about the design of the component your company is producing. Putting the details in an attachment may mean that senior management never sees them. (We'll talk later about how to structure your message to make sure the most important points get through, but for now we're limiting our consideration to the level and amount of detail appropriate for the different types of audience.)

Here are some guidelines to help you slant your writing to people who are uninformed or unfamiliar with your topic:

1. **Start with the key point the reader will want to know.** Why is this information important? What makes it relevant? What broad organizational implications does it have? Start by answering these questions and you're more likely to hook the uninformed audience. The point is to show that what you will describe or

discuss, the question you will ask, the opinion you will offer, is relevant to the reader's concerns and has a place within the reader's worldview. This positioning statement should make it easy for you to move from general to specific and from familiar to unique.

2. **Limit the technical content to what the reader absolutely needs to know.** Avoid digressions into technical details or options, no matter how interesting they may be to you. Avoid giving the uninformed audience "extra" information—it is more likely to confuse than to impress.

3. **Illustrate your main points.** Graphics are great for the uninformed audience, as long as they're easy to understand. The charts and graphs you find in *USA Today* are great examples of what works for this level of audience. The stuff you see in the *Journal of the American Medical Association* or in specialized engineering journals, not so much. Communicate your key points whenever possible with bar and pie charts, simple flowcharts, photos, maps, organization charts, and similar kinds of diagrams. Scatter diagrams, complex Gantt charts, and similar complex illustrations will intimidate your readers rather than help them. Likewise, avoid equations, programming statements, schematics, complex decision trees, and other specialized examples or illustrations and resist the urge to include illustrations from technical manuals.

   Unfortunately, graphics can be hard to use in an e-mail message. A different type of illustration you can use there is the word picture. Metaphors, comparisons, analogies, examples, and anecdotes are great ways to help the level one audience understand your point. Suppose you're an IT specialist, trying to explain to senior management why the company's information networks have been running so slowly. You've discovered that a lot of employees are running applications based on BitTorrent technology, which means they are draining huge amounts of computing power. Rather than try to explain that BitTorrent is a peer-to-peer protocol often used to transfer video and audio files, all of which is kind of interesting but irrelevant and possibly too technical, you might try an analogy:

What is happening to our network because of the BitTorrent applications is similar to what would happen if the water pipe delivering water to our house sprung multiple leaks. The water pressure would be terrible, and our bill would be sky high. Plugging the leaks—in this case, removing BitTorrent applications—will free up capacity and improve response times.

4. **Avoid using in-house jargon and keep your use of acronyms to a minimum.** This principle is probably self-explanatory. Don't forget that for this level of audience, the names of your products and services are jargon, too. You may know what the DSN2100 system is, but people outside the company probably don't.

   If you must use an acronym, define it. You may have been taught that the first time you use an acronym, you should present it in words and then put the acronym in parentheses immediately after the words. You might write something like this: "We have sales and support offices throughout Europe, the Middle East, and Africa (EMEA) to support clients of Abecedarian Avionics." But often that is not enough, because the words themselves may not make any sense to a level one reader. Sometimes you need to explain the concept in simple terms first, then name it in words, and finally introduce the acronym. Here are two versions. Which one do you think is more appropriate for the uninformed audience?

Voice over IP (VoIP) is an attractive option for our new phone system because it would dramatically cut what we spend for international calls. We would be able to call our offices in Copenhagen and Sydney at the same price we call locally.

Recent technical innovations that have made it possible to transmit telephone conversations over the Web could eliminate our long distance fees. Recently, this technology, known as Voice over IP [internet protocol] or VoIP, has matured to the point that it is a reasonable option for our company's phone system. Just as there's no special fee to view a Web site hosted in Copenhagen or Sydney, there's no special charge for placing a VoIP call to those places.

5. **Keep the words and the sentences simple and short.** We talked about this principle in terms of its positive impact on clarity. Clarity is particularly important for the uninformed audience. Use everyday language, mainly words of one and two syllables. Keep your sentences short and uncomplicated. Give yourself permission to write simply.

6. **Avoid referring the reader to specialized reports, manuals, or sources.** This level of reader won't look for them, probably wouldn't understand them, and possibly doesn't care. Your message to the uninformed reader must stand alone as a complete, self-contained document.

7. **Break down processes and procedures into a simple steps.** Start each description of a process with a simple explanation of what the process is and why it matters. Then go through the steps of the process chronologically. Number each step.

8. **Highlight your main points, make the transitions obvious, and reinforce your message with design and typography.** Most business readers skim, but none more so than the senior executives and mid-level managers from other business functions who are likely to make up a large portion of your uninformed audience. So make your document easy to skim. Use boldface type, headings, bullet points, color, white space, tint blocks, borders, and anything else that makes your key points jump off the page. We discussed earlier that with e-mail, some of these features may not be available at all or may disappear when your message goes from your e-mail system to the reader's, so it's equally important to make the logical structure of your message obvious by using transition words and phrases and by building your message on recognizable structural patterns. We'll talk about structural patterns in more detail in the next section on suitability for purpose.

The well-informed audience.   This audience has extensive knowledge of your field, but possibly less knowledge of the specialized project, product, or service you are discussing. For example, a colleague in operations may know a lot about your material handling systems, but may not possess any details about the new, photoelectric measurement tools you are introducing in the quality lab. An

MIS or IT manager may be very knowledgeable about LANs, WANs, and corporate database administration, but may not be aware of the specific features of the portal design you plan to implement on a Websphere platform. Sometimes the audience for your message knows as much (or more) about your subject as you do. Your direct boss or a peer working in the same team may have extensive knowledge not only of your field, but detailed familiarity with all the latest work in that field, industry trends, corporate objectives, and so on. However, before you decide that someone is an expert, please remember my warning that we all tend to overestimate our audience's level of understanding. If you aim for too high a level of expertise, your message will inevitably fail to communicate.

When you really do have a true expert audience, your writing task is much easier. It's not much different from sitting around the lunchroom table and talking with your own colleagues. You're just doing it in print with a little more formality and fewer sandwich crumbs.

The guidelines:

1. **Challenge yourself as you write.** The temptation when writing to a knowledgeable audience is to lapse into discursive, unfocused writing, to use jargon, to go off on tangents, to dwell on details for their own sake without indicating their significance. But that won't work. Even though this audience is very well informed, you must show that your message is relevant.
2. **Get right to the point.** Messages written to a well-informed audience should be extremely short and direct. If you need to provide more than a sentence of background, they're not well informed.
3. **Focus on the new or unique aspects of your message.** This is particularly true if you are writing one in a series of messages— a weekly or monthly project update, for example. You can assume the well-informed audience is already familiar with the basics of the project. What they need to know is what tasks have been completed since the last report, what new challenges you face, what milestones have been completed. Rehashing the basic purpose of the project or going through its history up to the point of your latest report wastes their time.

4. **Maintain your objectivity and use a professional tone.** Just because you're writing to people who are your colleagues, your peers, perhaps even your good friends, you can't lapse into sloppiness, slang, or the kind of writing we'd expect high school kids to be swapping back and forth via text messaging. Even if your recipient doesn't mind you writing that way, what happens if your message has to be passed up the chain of command?

5. **Use jargon (but be judicious).** Even for an expert, encountering a slew of acronyms and jargon makes for a distasteful reading experience. More than two or three acronyms in a sentence is usually difficult to read, even for an expert.

6. **Establish immediate links between the familiar and the new.** Suppose you have been asked to evaluate whether the company should outsource facility management services. If you know that your firm already contracts with someone to operate the corporate cafeteria, you can draw a parallel between that specific niche and the idea of turning over complete management of the facilities, including maintenance, security, landscaping, and other functions to outside firms.

Adjusting for Personality Type   The other factor to consider when analyzing your reader is his or her personality type. People are born with certain traits and preferences bound right into their double helix. Some of these inborn characteristics include the way they like to gather information, how they prefer to analyze it, and the ways they are most comfortable discussing it. If you know a bit about your audience's innate thinking and communicating style, you can deliver your message in the most effective way.

If you have dealt with the person to whom you are writing in a face-to-face situation, you probably already have insight into his or her preferences. How does she typically talk? Is he direct and focused on business? Does he like to interact socially first, talking about family or vacations or sports? Does she readily share feelings and communicate her own emotions? What does his work environment look like? Is it an undecorated cubicle or does it look like a teenager's bedroom with posters and pictures on all the flat surfaces? Has he hung schematics of jet engines on the wall or pictures of the kids? Certificates of accomplishment or birthday cards? The kind of information you need is the kind you can garner from simply observing how people talk and how they choose to create their own space. Even if you only talk with them over the phone, you can probably gain a lot of insight from listening to the people's manner of speaking. In your conversations, what really seems to matter to them? The more you learn about your audience, the more effectively and comfortably you will be able to write to them.

There are three questions in particular that can help you effectively slant your message to your readers.

1. Do they prefer an overview of the facts, or do they want them in depth?
2. Do they want to move quickly and get the key message in half a page, or do they prefer to move at a more deliberate pace and look at a longer presentation?
3. Are they interested strictly in measurable impact, or are they also interested in such factors as morale, job satisfaction, and similar "soft" factors?

Readers who would choose the first of each pair listed above are pragmatic, bottom-line people who are oriented toward action and results. They are not interested in having all the facts, just the ones that help them make a decision or move forward quickly. If you give them too much detail (and it doesn't take much for them to think it's "too much"), you will irritate them. They want you to be concise, focused, and businesslike in your writing. They want you to focus on facts, ideas, and evidence, not feelings or people. They admire precision, efficiency, and a well-organized delivery in both written and oral communications. The quickest way to irritate these readers is to take a long time to get to the point. They're constantly asking, "So what? Why does this matter to me? What's the value here?"

Very early in my career I wrote speeches for the vice president of international sales for Procter & Gamble, a man named Lou Pritchett. He was a very influential figure in P&G's history, since he personally took Sam Walton out fishing in a rowboat one day so they could negotiate one-on-one to get P&G's products into Wal-Mart stores. Lou was born and raised in the deep South and spoke with a charming Southern accent, but his mind was laser sharp. When you'd meet with him on a project, he would always welcome you warmly: "Well, hello, Tom, it's just wonderful to see you again. I hope you're doing well? Glad to hear it, Tom. Well, I've got a couple of minutes free right now, so what is it I can do for you?" The key phrase in all of that was "a couple of minutes." If you didn't get to the point within the first two minutes and show Lou that it was a point he was interested in, he would slowly rise from his desk, smiling warmly, and put his arm around your shoulders and gently shove you out the door. Just to show you that he was consistent in this regard, he refused to write or read any memos that were longer than one page. Can you imagine the impact a project update written by a highly technical and detailed author, one that rambled on for four or five pages, would have on a reader like Lou Pritchett?

One the other hand, some of your readers will be like that author of the detailed, lengthy project summary. These folks prefer to get the facts in depth, presented at a careful, deliberate pace. They want any discussion of impact to be measurable, evidence based, and objective. Using Fluff and Weasel will be particularly irritating to these readers, because hype and marketing buzz arouse their suspicion. They highly value accuracy and thoroughness, so they expect and actually welcome more detail than other readers typically will, but they dislike and are often uncomfortable with the use of emotional terms and inexact language. They like to know how things work, what all of the features are, what the technical options might be. When they read your document (or listen to your oral presentation), they want to know how things work and how they can logically justify any decisions. I remember a leading consultant with one of the major accounting firms laughing as he told me that CPAs were the worst possible audience for him, even though he was one himself. "You can be providing a very useful overview of changes in tax law, for example, and if down in the corner of your slide you have two numbers that don't add up correctly, the audience will immediately discount everything you say. In fact, they won't even hear it, because they'll be too busy recalculating all the other numbers to see if you made any other mistakes."

People who prefer to get the facts in depth, at a deliberate pace, focused on measures of impact that are qualitative as well as quantitative, are people who care about how others will respond. They value warm, personal relationships and will look for a message that also seems to share those values. At the least, they expect your message to be written in a way that communicates rapport, personal interest, and genuineness. They want you to be dependable and reliable. Consensus seekers often have flashes of insight into you as an individual and into your meaning, and they're likely to pick up inconsistencies between your apparent message and your hidden intentions. Unfortunately, they're also likely to garble technical or factual data, make erroneous assumptions, or introduce unwanted emotional messages. As a result, it's very difficult for a highly analytical thinker and writer to communicate successfully with this kind of reader, and vice versa.

What should you do if you are writing to a group of people? Design your message in terms of two parts—an opening component and a detailed component. In the opening component of your message, which might be as short as a single paragraph or as long as two or three pages, address the bottom-line issues that bottom-line, pragmatic readers care about. Put a heading on this part, something like "Overview of the Business Issues." Then go into detail in the second part of your message, writing as though your audience were the analytical type. This section should also have a heading. You could call it "Details and Discussion of Next Steps" or something like that to suggest which kind of reader it's designed to suit.

Sometimes a person's job requires him or her to act like a certain type of person even though that's in conflict with his or her true personality. A high-level executive almost always has to think "pragmatically," and a person with technical responsibilities may have to adopt an "analytical" approach. Should you write to the "real" person or the "role" person? The answer depends on whether you're trying to inform or persuade. Information will be most acceptable if it's structured for the role; persuasion will be most successful if it's pitched to the real.

I don't want you to worry about this too much. Just be aware of the broad lineaments of personality and their impact on reading preferences. And it would help if you had some insight into your own personality and what you prefer, because you are most likely to produce a document that is exactly like the kind of document you would like to receive. Unfortunately, it may not be the kind your audience wants. It's another example of the importance of getting outside our own head and into the head of our reader in order to communicate more effectively.

Suitability for the Purpose

Students are seldom taught about the importance of structure in writing. They may get some exposure to it in the form of certain kinds of essays they write in freshman English class, but beyond that they seldom get any useful training unless they go into a specialized field, like journalism. That's a pity, because structure is more important than style for successful writing. You can write your report or e-mail in bullet points, using nothing but phrases and fragments, and the reader will find it acceptable if it delivers the content in the right pattern. On the other hand, you can write like Dickens or Dostoevsky, but if your pattern is wrong, the results will be wrong. The reader will finish reading what you wrote and be dissatisfied with the experience.

Over the years, I've come to believe that the worst mistakes in business communication have nothing to do with grammar or spelling or sentence complexity. Instead, they stem from using the wrong structural pattern, one that is not capable of achieving our purpose. For example, if we deliver flat, accurate, factual content, thinking that the facts alone will persuade our customer to buy, we have profoundly misunderstood the way communication works.

Suppose that Tiger Woods were to stride to the first tee in a major tournament, tee his ball up just so, execute a couple of careful practice swings before addressing the ball, and then whack it as hard as he could with his putter. No matter how perfectly he hits the ball, the results won't be quite right. He's using the wrong tool for the job. He has used a club designed to roll the ball across the green with precision in an effort to launch it several hundred yards down the fairway, and it's not likely to work very well. Something similar will happen if you use a pattern that's not suited to your purpose. For example, if you use an informative structural pattern to deliver a persuasive message, or vice versa, you will confuse the reader, muddle the message by miscommunicating your intent, and not get the results you want.

Structure is important at the level of the sentence, the paragraph, and the document as a whole. We've already discussed some of the important elements of good sentence structure in our section on clarity. There's no question that short, simple sentences are easier to read than long, complicated sentences full of obscure language strung together on a rickety framework of passive voice verbs. But even if we write absolutely beautiful sentences, each a little jewel of English prose in its own right, we still might fail to communicate effectively. A string of well-written sentences doesn't add up to a good report, a compelling proposal, or even a meaningful memo. The sentences need to be organized into coherent paragraphs that serve a broader purpose. And those paragraphs need to be combined into a document that follows the pattern that's most effective for achieving our intention in writing. Let's take a look at those aspects of the language of success next: paragraph and document structure.

Paragraphs: The Building Blocks of Thought   If you understand how to put a paragraph together, you can deliver a message that sounds much more coherent and logical than the vast majority of writing we encounter every day. In this section, we'll spend some time looking at paragraph structures before we turn our attention to the broader patterns appropriate for information, evaluation, and persuasion.

What is a paragraph? It's a unit of writing that consists of one or more sentences. Think of the paragraphs as building blocks or a kind of language-based Lego. Just as Legos come in different shapes, allowing us to fit them together to make cool overall structures—a pirate ship or a castle or a jet fighter—we can choose from different "shapes" of paragraphs and assemble them into coherent messages.

I said in the previous paragraph that a paragraph can consist of one or more sentences. A few of you may have winced at that, because you were taught back in the eighth grade—as I was, may I add—that a paragraph must have a certain minimum number of sentences. The most frequently cited number is five, and those five sentences supposedly have very specific roles within the paragraph.

Sentence one is the topic sentence, announcing the subject. Sentence two is a restatement of the theme. I guess the purpose of that one is to make sure your reader didn't miss the point the first time it went by, but it always struck me as redundant. The next two sentences, numbers three and four, are examples to explain our topic. Sentence five is our summary and transition into the next paragraph. How precise, how clear, and how utterly mechanical. Have you ever read anything written that way? It's like novocaine in print. In reality, I didn't buy it back when my teacher was teaching it to us, and I don't buy it now. I honestly believe that the right answer to the question *How long should a paragraph be?* is that it should be as long as it needs to be to make a clear point and no longer. That's why once sentence may be enough.

A more useful concept is this: You can build your paragraphs on a range of different logical principles. The inherent logic of your paragraph structures will impart additional clarity to your writing if you choose them carefully.

Most people don't think about how they organize their paragraphs. Instead, their controlling pattern is stream of consciousness. Whatever thoughts pop into their heads next, that's what goes on the page. When there's a chunk of text that looks large enough, they hit the return key and start creating a new paragraph. Writing this way is analogous to taking the Legos out the box at random and just stacking them up next to each other. The process isn't going to add up to much at the end, is it? No cool pirate ship, no police car, nothing. Just a pile of blocks.

Because of this stream-of-consciousness technique, the underlying pattern in most paragraphs is a kind of crude chronology. First this happened, then that, then this other thing, then something else. When we're describing a process or a chain of events, chronology might be tolerable. When we're doing something a bit more sophisticated, it will fail miserably.

Suppose you are a unit manager in an engineering firm and you just attended a planning session with your division head and the other unit managers. And suppose you got the following e-mail from the division head shortly after the session had concluded:

TO: All attendees
FROM: Liz Duckabi
SUBJECT: Following up

Thanks everybody for a great session. I felt exhausted yet exhilirated (sp?) at the end, and I have to say the weather was perfect. It was kind of a shame we had to spend so much of our time indoors, but all the same it was worth it. We covered a lot of ground, didn't we? Anyway, one of the issues we discussed in regards to our planning for next year is the consolidation of work processes across units, including tools. Each of you has had success in managing your own segment of the business and your projects, but as we discussed it could help lower costs and give us some leverage if we could consolidate on a few basic tools. With that in mind, would you please get back to me with a list of the specific software applications you're using? Just audit what you use in the course of a typical project, everything from say Word and Excel all the way to any specific analytical tools, graphics packages, drafting, etc etc. I'd like to have your list in the next couple of days. Once we're back, we'll have plenty to do to catch up, but this is an area where I think quick follow up will be beneficial. Maybe there won't be a real opportunity for consolidation or whatever, but if there is, then the sooner we take advantage of it, the sooner we can start saving.

Thanks!

Liz

It's pretty clear that Liz just sat down and started pecking away on her keyboard without giving much thought to what she was about to say. She didn't even bother to check the spelling of *exhilarated*. It's hard to take her request seriously, and if I started reading it quickly, based on the pointless subject line and the drawn out opening, I might never notice she's asking for a response from me in the next 48 hours. Her entire e-mail is one paragraph, which is fine, but the organizational pattern for that paragraph is the kind of stream of consciousness we all see way too often. Liz—get to the point. Get focused! Stop wasting my time.

What if she wrote her message to us like this?

TO: All attendees
FROM: Liz Duckabi
SUBJECT: Establishing a list of commonly used tools and processes

One of the most exciting ideas to come out of our planning meeting was the one about consolidating and standardizing at least some of our work processes and tools. The first step toward determining if that will actually save us money is to identify what we're all using. Please send me a list of the specific software packages you and your teams use in the course of a project. Include everything from basic office applications all the way to the most specialized tools. Please get the list to me by the close of business Wednesday. I'll consolidate the information and share it with you as soon as possible. Then we can make some decisions.

Thanks,

Liz

If she writes the e-mail that way, we get the point quicker, we do less reading, and we are much less likely to not respond on time. It might be even better if she enumerated her request so that it stands out more, like this:

. . . The first step toward determining if that will actually save us money is to identify what we're all using. Accordingly, please:

1. Send me a list of the specific software packages you and your teams use in the course of a project.
2. Include everything from basic office applications all the way to the most specialized tools.
3. Get the list to me by the close of business Wednesday.

I'll consolidate the information and share it with you as soon as possible. Then we can make some decisions.

When we change the formatting to enumerate each step of her request, the pattern of the paragraph becomes more obvious. We've gone from randomness to order by writing a simple process description. That's one of the patterns you can use to make your writing more readable.

Chronology is a basic pattern that builds on our everyday experience of seeing events unfold in time. Basically, chronological order is a way of telling a story. All of the content proceeds in a temporal sequence:

> Last week's visit to our "big four" schools for recruiting interviews was quite successful in spite of transportation problems at the end of the week. On Tuesday, we visited Harvard and conducted 12 half-hour interviews in the course of 9 hours. We identified three candidates we will invite to our offices for second-tier interviews. On Wednesday, we were at NYU. We had 7 interviews and identified two candidates to invite. On Thursday we interviewed 10 students at Columbia and will invite three of them. Unfortunately, a freak snowstorm hit the New York area Thursday night, grounding all flights, so we missed our opportunity to visit the Cornell campus. The Cornell coordinator indicated she will look for an opportunity to reschedule us next month.

You can see that this paragraph starts with a general topic sentence and then moves forward, using the days of the week and the different campuses to organize the details. It's not the most interesting piece of writing, but it's clear enough. We could make it even easier to understand if we restructured the whole thing as a table:

> Here is a summary of our recruiting interviews last week at the "big four" schools:
>
> | Tuesday | Wednesday | Thursday | Friday |
> |---|---|---|---|
> | Harvard | NYU | Columbia | Cornell— |
> | 12 interviews | 7 interviews | 10 interviews | CANCELLED |
> | 3 invites | 2 invites | 3 invites | (weather) |
>
> We will reschedule the Cornell visit for next month.

The contrast between the original version and the reorganized version shows that chronological order, while logical and clear, isn't necessarily the best way to organize information. It often requires a lot more words to communicate the key points. In fact, as a general rule, when you organize your content chronologically, your writing is almost always wordier than it has to be. When I encounter it in my clients' writing, I often look for a simpler, more effective way of organizing the content. Sometimes chronological order is the best choice, but it's often a lazy way of gaining order without much thought.

Key point with details.   Another paragraph pattern, perhaps the one that we think of as the "classic" pattern for developing paragraphs, is the topic sentence plus details. The details might be facts, examples, or some other form of proof. The first sentence in the paragraph, the topic sentence, states the main point, in a succinct, general way. That point is then developed or further explained through a sequence of facts, statistics, quotes, anecdotes, or other forms of evidence. Here's an example of this kind of pattern:

> The sheer complexity of warehousing, shipping, and distribution in the apparel industry is staggering. Consider, for example, the volume of items that a typical manufacturer of athletic footwear and clothing moves through the supply chain. Each year a single manufacturer will ship, store, and distribute into the retail network more than 40 million pieces of apparel. At the same time, the same firm will move nearly 50 million pairs of shoes. In addition, most of the major players in this industry will offer specific styles and designs in conjunction with key marketing events, such as the World Series, which must hit the stores at exactly the right moment. All in all, it represents a huge logistics challenge.

Descriptions—either spatial or sequential.   A frequent task for writers in a business setting is to describe something—a process, a piece of equipment, or a facility, for example. We describe processes when we explain how to perform a task (how to calibrate a piece of laboratory equipment) or how an event happens or will happen (the formation of mold on the interior walls of buildings; the sequence of activities planned for our user conference). When you describe a process, you can structure the paragraph by starting with a topic sentence that defines what the process is, a second sentence (if you need it) that indicates why the process matters, and then the sequence of steps or phases of the event presented using the chronological pattern.

In light of recent changes in the home mortgage market, we have started a project to review alternative approaches to creating investment vehicles that are aimed at assisting first-time buyers and delivering significant yield for investors. This work is being led by the Urban Finance Initiative team and is intended to determine (1) if our current first-time buyer products, or some variation of those products, are properly designed for today's market and (2) if they will attract sufficient private sector investment to allow us to expand them. To analyze these two issues we will perform three tasks. First, we will analyze the discounted cash flow model developed for our original first-time buyer program. From this analysis we hope to gain a clear understanding of the key drivers in the model and whether recent economic changes require us to modify it. Second, we will develop some options for private sector investment. As part of this development effort we will look at new products being developed by our competitors to determine if our options are likely to be competitive in today's market. If necessary, we will modify our options to maximize their appeal to private sector investors. Third, we will undertake a series of market tests, approaching a predefined list of private sector investors, including both banks and pension funds. The market tests will give us a clear indication of the total potential of our new fund vehicles.

Admittedly, this is a fairly complex paragraph. You can see how it follows the pattern I outlined, from the topic sentence through the clarification of purpose for the process and to the presentation of the phases of activity. The structure is sound and logical. However, there's a lot to digest here. We could make the reader's job even easier if we use some formatting to cluster the various components on the page:

In light of recent changes in the home mortgage market, we have started a project to review alternative approaches to creating investment vehicles that are aimed at assisting first-time buyers and delivering significant yield for investors. This work is being led by the Urban Finance Initiative team and is intended to determine

(1) if our current first-time buyer products, or some variation of those products, are properly designed for today's market and
(2) if they will attract sufficient private sector investment to allow us to expand them.

To analyze these two issues we will perform three tasks.

First, we will analyze the discounted cash flow model developed for our original first-time buyer program. From this analysis we hope to gain a clear understanding of the key drivers in the model and whether recent economic changes require us to modify it.

Second, we will develop some options for private sector investment. As part of this development effort we will look at new products being developed by our competitors to determine if our options are likely to be competitive in today's market. If necessary, we will modify our options to maximize their appeal to private sector investors.

Third, we will undertake a series of market tests, approaching a predefined list of private sector investors, including both banks and pension funds. The market tests will give us a clear indication of the total potential of our new fund vehicles.

To provide a coherent description of a physical object, start with a topic sentence that identifies the object—the piece of equipment, the facility, the building site, or whatever it is you're writing about. After you've identified it, describe its component parts in a consistent spatial order. For example, depending on what you're writing about, you might be able to describe the object from top to bottom or from left to right. Before you start your spatial description, you might want to orient the reader to the point of view from which you are looking at the object. Are we standing in front of the machine? To the side? Taking a bird's-eye view? A graphic will be extremely useful for most readers, particularly if they're one of those uninformed audiences not familiar with your subject matter. By the way, if you're describing a piece of equipment, you also have the option of describing its component parts sequentially in the order they are used in a typical cycle of operation. Here's an example of a spatially organized description of a building. Although you've never seen the building, I'll bet you could draw a pretty good picture of it after you read this paragraph:

> The truck assembly plant is located 20 kilometers outside of Stockholm and is used for both manufacturing and administrative purposes. The building is shaped like a letter T, although a T with a very short base and a very wide crossbar. The base of the T houses all of the administrative offices in a two-story building. Finance and accounting are on the lower floor, and sales, customer support, and general management are on the upper floor. The actual assembly work is carried out in the cross-bar of the T, a facility that extends nearly 300 meters from one end to the other. The basic truck chassis enters at the left end of the T and from there moves down a linear assembly line, where the engine, drive train, cab, and other components are added. Although more than 30 years old, the facility is still quite efficient and, given its straightforward design, has proven to be easy to update.

Comparison and/or contrast.   If you are writing an evaluative document, you may find that you need to compare or contrast two or more things. There are two ways to structure a comparison/contrast paragraph. One pattern is to start with a topic sentence that defines what you are writing about and then proceeds to give all the details about the first object, all of the details about the second, and so on. You discuss each item that you are comparing or contrasting by itself completely before moving on to the next item. The other way to structure this kind of paragraph is to alternate the details. You start with a topic sentence again, then you discuss a detail as it pertains to item one, item two, and so on. Then you discuss a different detail as it pertains to item one, item two, and so on. You continue this pattern until you have discussed all the details. They both work. This paragraph that you are reading right now is an example of the first kind of structural pattern. I described one way of organizing the comparison/contract paragraph completely, then I described the other way to do it. Here's an example that alternates the details:

One of the choices we face is whether to buy the software we need or to have our IT staff build it. Both approaches have strengths and weakness in terms of business fit, costs, and speed of delivery. In terms of business fit, commercial software available through any of several large software providers will have the basic functions we need to track our key performance indicators. On the other hand, a custom-built application can be designed around our actual business processes, making it easier to generate the reports and to do the drill down we need. The costs of the two approaches are quite different. Commercial software, by its nature, takes advantage of economies of scale. We would be able to get a complete package for all of our users, a full installation and support package of services, and training for under a million dollars. A custom development project of this magnitude will involve three to four full-time developers, one system architect, a project manager, and, on an occasional basis, testers, technical writers, and trainers. Because we would have in depth knowledge of the system in house, installation and maintenance would simply require assigning a few dedicated resources. We estimate total costs for the development project and the first year of operation to be about $2.5 million. Thereafter, the cost of ownership will be about half what we would pay in maintenance fees for a commercial application. Finally, in terms of speed of delivering a fully functioning system, commercial software can be installed and operating in six months. As noted, building this application ourselves will be a major undertaking that we estimate will last 18 months. In summary, although we would sacrifice some degree of business fit by going with a commercial product, the acquisition costs and speed of delivery all favor using a commercially available application.

You're probably already thinking that this paragraph could be formatted so that it's even easier to understand. If we group the three factors used to compare commercial software with custom-built software, we can provide our reader with a clear indication of structure:

One of the choices we face is whether to buy the software we need or to have our IT staff build it. Both approaches have strengths and weakness in terms of business fit, costs, and speed of delivery.

Business fit
Commercial software: The systems available through any of several large software providers will have the basic functions we need to track our key performance indicators.

Custom built software: In contrast, we can design our own application around our actual business processes, making it easier to generate the reports and to do the drill down we need.

Costs
Commercial software, by its nature, takes advantage of economies of scale. We would be able to get a complete package for all of our users, a full installation and support package of services, and training for under a million dollars.

Custom-built software: A custom development project of this magnitude will involve three to four full-time developers, one system architect, a project manager, and, on an occasional basis, testers, technical writers, and trainers. Because we would have in depth knowledge of the system in house, installation and maintenance would simply require assigning a few dedicated resources. We estimate total costs for the development project and the first year of operation to be about $2.5 million. Thereafter, the cost of ownership will be about half what we would pay in maintenance fees for a commercial application.

Speed of delivery
Commercial: Finally, in terms of speed of delivering a fully functioning system, commercial software can be installed and operating in six months.

Custom-built: As noted, building this application ourselves will be a major undertaking that we estimate will last 18 months.

In summary, although we would sacrifice some degree of business fit by going with a commercial product, the acquisition costs and speed of delivery all favor using a commercially available application.

The second version takes up more room on the page, but it's easier to read. The indentations, bold type, and underlining all make it easier for us to find our way through the pattern.

Definition.   Another frequent task for business writers is defining terms. Sometimes we just need to make sure everyone is using terminology the same way. Sometimes we might be trying to change our reader's assumptions or perceptions about a topic, moving him or her away from preconceived notions toward a new view that's more favorable for us. The following paragraph is meant to define a term while simultaneously creating a favorable impression of the process to which the term applies:

Another term you may encounter in federal procurement policies is "cost realism." One way to define cost realism is to see it as an attempt by government acquisition specialists to gain a reality check on the price quotes vendors submit in response to federal RFPs. To achieve cost realism, contract administrators are encouraged to create a "competitive range" chart, in which they group all of the prices received from all vendors. Those prices that are significantly above or below the "competitive range" of pricing are thrown out as being unrealistic. This process helps avoid the problem of awarding a contract to a vendor who has "low balled" the project in order to win with the intention of making a profit on change orders and cost overruns. It also avoids the problem of choosing a solution that is overdesigned and over-engineered to the point that the government ends up paying $500 for a hammer.

Classification.   Classification is the process of dividing something up into component parts or of figuring out which predefined category something belongs in. It helps people relate something new to something they already understand. In the following paragraph, we are classifying storage procedures into two categories and explaining a bit about each.

Methods for storing solid waste generated from nuclear power plants fall into two categories—short-term solutions and long-term. Of course, since we are talking about waste products that must be stored more than 10,000 years, the concepts of short-term and long-term are relative. Short-term means decades, while long-term literally means millennia. Currently, short-term storage of spent fuel rods involves placing the rods in pools of water for several years or decades, until they have "cooled" sufficiently to be moved into a second phase of short-term storage, encasement inside steel and concrete casks. Short-term storage is handled on the site of the nuclear power plant. However, because a typical nuclear power plant produces 25 to 30 tons of spent fuel rods a year, these short-term measures must be supplemented by a long-term option that gets the waste products off the site of the nuclear facility. Otherwise, all of the land will quickly be taken up storing spent fuel. Unfortunately, long-term storage remains the most controversial part of the process, since no one wants to have highly radioactive waste materials stored in their locale. Original plans to store nuclear fuel for 10,000 years in deep tunnels inside the Yucca Mountain range in Nevada are currently on hold.

Cause and effect.   You can organize a paragraph by starting with some important event, decision, or other focusing element and then tracing all the effects and consequences related to it. Or you can do it the other way, starting with a single effect or phenomenon and moving backward to identify all the factors that caused it.

Fourth quarter sales of scooters, particularly the Vespa line, were up by 42% over the previous quarter and were more than double the same quarter last year. I believe there were three main reasons for this terrific performance. First, we had some unseasonably warm weather, which extended our "buying season" well into late November. Second, our promotion of Bike Safety Day at Farmer's Market generated a lot of leads. Third, our new policy of letting people buy a scooter with their credit card eliminated some of the delays we had in the past with getting bank financing.

Question and answer.   This pattern is easy to understand. Your topic sentence consists of a question—the fabled "rhetorical question" we've all heard about—and then proceeds to answer it.

> Should we add relocation support to our mix of employee benefits? Given the nature of our business, we will continue to transfer employees, particularly at the middle management level, an average of once every three to four years. Relocation can be traumatic for an employee and his or her family, even more so if they are left to their own devices to sell their house, find a new one, set up the move, and handle all the details involved in starting life over in a new city. Finding good employees in today's market is extremely difficult, which means keeping the ones we have is vital. In my opinion, we can reduce stress and increase loyalty by establishing a relocation benefit as part of our employee benefit package.

Purposes and Patterns for the Whole Message

As we've already discussed, we need to know *why* we are writing so that we know *how* to write. We need to understand our *purpose* so we can select the right *pattern*.

When we write to an audience, there is an implicit contract between us. We promise to communicate in a way that they understand and find useful; they promise to give our message enough attention to understand it. Entering into that implicit contract means we both have to have the same goal in mind. They need some information so they can complete a task. We understand that and attempt to deliver the information they need as clearly and concisely as possible. They want to know our opinion on some matter where we have relevant expertise. We understand that and try to provide our opinion in a way that shows the logic behind our thinking. They want to make a decision. We understand and write persuasively.

When we write, we need to know how our audience will use the content we are providing. If we fail to ask that basic question, we are likely to lapse into doing what we like to do. And for almost everyone, the purpose they are most comfortable handling is providing information. Putting down the facts that somebody else needs to do his or her job is a task most of feel we can handle pretty well.

Writing to evaluate—to provide facts that lead up to an expression of our opinion about what those facts mean—is more difficult for most people. If the evaluation involves doing something awkward or if it involves handling touchy material, such as a performance appraisal might, we may actually dread doing it. Finally, writing to motivate or persuade others is extremely difficult. At the outset of this book, we looked at two horrific examples of e-mails sent out by CEOs whose apparent intent was to motivate employees but who produced the opposite reaction. Persuasion is the most difficult form of business writing.

Each of these purposes is legitimate. Each has its place in business writing. And, most important, each has a specific pattern for developing the content that will work most effectively. Research in cognitive linguistics has shown that our brains are hardwired to receive and process content differently, depending on what we're trying to do with it. If we're just trying to absorb it so we can use it later, we're looking for a pattern of organization that facilitates the transfer of information. On the other hand, if we're trying to make a buying decision, we're looking for a pattern of development that facilitates decision making—a persuasive structure. If we use the wrong pattern, we doom our efforts to almost certain failure. We're teeing off with a putter in our hands!

This is an aspect of writing that separates it from spoken language. Although some speakers are capable of spinning out rather complex thoughts, speaking in fully developed ideas and examples, nobody regularly speaks in paragraphs. Instead, speaking is a two-way process, involving the speaker and the audience, in a kind of dance. Most of the time the speaker leads, but sometimes the audience—through a facial expression, a bit of body language, a brief interjection ("Sure!" "Right . . . " "Wait, who said that?")—redirects the steps of the dance so both partners stay connected. We can't do that in writing, of course, which is why our written language is much more tightly controlled.

Research into linguistics has helped explain how language works and has shed insight on the issue of structure aligning with purpose. Any time we communicate, six elements must be present and working in concert for the message to make any sense. The six elements are sender, receiver, subject, form, code, and contact. Their relationship to each other is illustrated in Figure 3.3. Trust me, gaining a bit of insight into these six elements and how they combine to make communication work will help you understand the linkage between purpose and structure.

Let's start with the two most basic elements—the sender and the receiver. The sender is the person who is writing the e-mail, delivering the presentation, gesturing, grimacing, or otherwise engaging in an act of communication. The **receiver** is the person or group of people who reads the e-mail or letter or project plan or proposal, who watches the pitch, who observes the body language.

The solid arrow indicates the main way communication flows: You send a message; the audience receives it. The dotted arrow heading in the reverse direction represents a feedback loop, something we can take advantage of when we're presenting directly to the audience. We can see their reactions in the form of facial expressions, arms crossed, slumped or tense postures, gestures, and maybe even verbal behavior on the part of the receiver, such as questions or interruptions. As I mentioned earlier, the lack of an immediate feedback loop is one reason it's so much harder to write than to speak. And it's a very good reason why you should write a draft of any important messages and ask someone who is similar to your intended audience to read it. Ask her if it's clear, if it makes sense, if it seems complete. On major proposal efforts, the proposal manager will often schedule something called a Red Team review, which is basically just a matter of getting a lot of people together to read and score the draft proposal. It helps improve the final draft because it provides the feedback loop in advance of actually publishing the document.

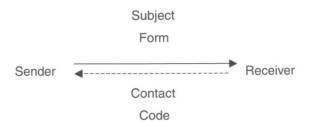

Figure 3.3   The six elements necessary for communication to occur.

The **subject** is the topic you're writing about. You might be summarizing last month's shipment figures, or recommending a change to our hiring policy, or trying to persuade me that our warehousing system needs to be replaced. Assuming that we both use language in standard ways and that neither of us is actively hallucinating, there's a good chance that your message will provoke thoughts and mental imagery in me that is reasonably close to the thoughts and images you had when you wrote it. There will be some variation, based on our own experiences and on your choice of words. Vague, general words ("dog") will produce fuzzier images in the reader's head than more precise language ("dachshund"), but words that are too precise may creep into the realm of jargon and become incomprehensible.

The **sender, receiver,** and **subject** are clearly the basic elements of any communication. But the other three elements—**form, contact, and code**—also must be present or the communication will fail.

For example, the factor that I call *form* covers the way the document or spoken words are put together to create a specific kind of message. We use formal elements all the time without realizing it. For example, the next time your child asks you tell him or her a bedtime story, instead of "Once upon a time . . . " try starting it like this: "Fourth quarter results showed strong demand in the retail sector, but adverse performance of certain financial vehicles kept the CEO's company from achieving its targets. As a result, a mean dragon demanded that he hand over his daughter to pay off his company's debts." I'd be willing to bet that your child will look at you like you've lost it. The first sentence is the wrong "form" for a bedtime story, unless it's being told by Lou Dobbs. I doubt you'll make it more than halfway through that first sentence before your child starts to whine, "Daaaddddy [or Mommmmy], tell me a real story!"

You probably recall from English class that a sonnet always has fourteen lines and is written in iambic pentameter. You might remember that a haiku consists of three lines with a total of seventeen syllables distributed in a pattern of five, seven, and five. Those are extreme examples of communications that have rigidly defined forms. But the form of a business communication like a letter or a proposal can be almost as strict, and in the case of a response to a request for proposal, which contains specific guidelines on how to format and organize your response (perhaps even to the point of telling you which font to use and how many pages to write), the form is tightly controlled. Even the formal salutation that starts a letter ("Dear Mary,") is an element of form, showing that this is indeed a letter.

The term *contact* refers to the fact that we must open a channel of communication between us and our audience and keep that channel open. We need to attract the audience's attention and establish rapport quickly so that they will read what we write or listen to what we say.

Last, there's the *code* element, which means sharing the same language. The importance of sharing the code is pretty obvious if you've tried to do business in Latin America with a limited knowledge of Spanish, or if you've tried to sell products into the Far East without good fluency in the customer's language. But even among people who speak the same language, there can be problems. We've already discussed how damaging Geek can be—the use of technical terms and jargon that the audience doesn't understand. Other professions also have their own specialized code. In fact, it's easy to spot jargon when it's from a field other than our own. The challenge comes when we have to monitor our use of language from within our field.

All six elements—sender, receiver, message, form, contact, and code—must be present for a communication to occur. If one of them is missing, communication breaks down. But the other important point is that in every communication, one element dominates the others.

For example, to start with the simplest example, a dictionary focuses on the **code** element—it uses language to explain language. So does a nomenclature table or a list of acronyms in a technical manual.

Contact is often the dominant element in purely social activities. At a networking event people mill around, make small talk, maybe exchange business cards. The content of the communication looks negligible: "How are you? How do you like this weather? How 'bout them Cubs?" But the literal content of the exchanges isn't what matters. The whole point is establishing a bit of rapport, opening up a channel of communication you can follow up on later.

If the **form** of the communication is its most important element, you may be reading a work of literature. The form of a mystery novel helps determine the way we read it and how we react; the form of a half-hour situation comedy is as predictable as a haiku. Oddly enough, recognizing the form of a joke where we know the structure of what's coming (a punch line, a limerick) is part of the pleasure of hearing it.

However, in a business or professional setting, none of these elements is likely to dominate. Contact, code, and format are typically means to an end. Instead, the dominant elements of communication in a business setting are the **subject**, the **sender**, and the **receiver.**

When the **subject** is the controlling element, we are engaged in the job of communicating *information.* Our goal is to provide facts as clearly and concisely as possible so that someone else can understand those facts and use them to do his or her job:

> Here are the three steps necessary to submit your expense report.

> We have completed spectrographic analysis of the alloy samples, following thermal stress testing. Results indicate . . .

> We are pleased to announce that Pat Edwards has joined our staff as senior account manager. Pat will be responsible for Mettering Memorial Hospital as well as several large group practices.

If the dominant element is the **sender,** we are creating the kind of document whose purpose is to communicate our opinion. Typically, when we present facts and then offer our (presumably) informed opinion about what those facts mean, we are engaged in an act of *evaluation.* The focus is on us as the sender—as an expert or at least as somebody who has done a bit of research and thinking. For example, if you're a marketing manager, you might be asked by senior management to evaluate the various marketing activities the company has undertaken during the past twelve months and evaluate which ones were most effective. You might use a variety of criteria—cost of the activity, number of leads generated, long-term impact on brand recognition—but what management wants is your opinion. What do you think is working? What's not?

Finally, if the **audience** is the dominant element, you are engaged in an act of *persuasion*. When we combine facts and our opinions in such a way that we influence what the audience thinks, how they feel, or what they do, we are engaged in a form of communication in which the receiver is the most important component. Selling to customers, motivating employees, inspiring team effort: These are all persuasive activities that require a persuasive structure to be effective.

Writing to Inform

When people present facts that other people need to do their jobs, they're writing to inform. The goal of informative writing is to be concise and accurate. We measure the success of informative writing by how quickly and easily the facts are transferred from your head into mine. We consider the communication a failure if our reader doesn't understand the facts or, worse yet, misunderstands them.

The best way to communicate informatively is to use the pattern taught in journalism classes: the funnel. Start with the fact or set of facts that is most important to the reader. In journalism, that's often *who, what, when, where, why,* and *how*? Then go to the next most important fact. Then the third level of importance. The fourth, the fifth, and so on, until there is nothing left to say. By structuring your document this way, you allow your readers to stop reading as soon as they have seen enough.

The challenge in writing informatively is to figure out which fact is most important to the reader. If you were to go back and look at coverage of Martha Stewart's conviction for obstruction of justice, comparing the way it was reported in the *Wall Street Journal* with the way the same events were covered in *People,* you would see a dramatically different emphasis. The articles had very different opening paragraphs because they have very different readers. In one publication, the focus was on the fact that the conviction caused the stock price of Martha Stewart Living Omnimedia to drop over 20 percent; in the other, the emphasis was on the emotional reactions shown by

Stewart herself, her aged mother, and her daughter. Both publications got it right because they both know their readers so well. Readers understand that they will be dealt with differently, too. Many people read both *People* and the *Journal*, changing their mindsets and expectations as they lay one down and pick up the other.

The most common mistakes that people make when presenting information are writing chronologically, which usually leads to wordiness, or starting with facts that matter to the writer but not to the reader, which usually leads to confusion or false emphasis.

Writing to Evaluate

Sometimes people aren't trying to communicate facts alone. Instead, they're trying to interpret what those facts mean. They're offering an opinion about the significance of a certain group of facts, what those facts imply. This is particularly true when the facts are being offered in comparison to another set of related facts.

For example, consider what happens in a court case when one side calls in an expert witness. Such a witness isn't asked to establish facts about the case—"Where was the defendant on the night of July 15?" Instead, the expert witness is asked to offer an opinion about what a certain body of facts indicates. "On the basis of these facts, do you think the defendant is mentally competent?" "Given this sequence of events, did the defendant act in accord with the profession's current standard of conduct?"

In the business world, each time you write a performance appraisal or do a competitive analysis, you're writing an evaluation. If you merely recite the facts but don't offer your opinion, you aren't doing the whole job.

An evaluation can be compared to a hamburger, where you need a top bun (the introduction), a bottom bun (the conclusion), and lots of meat in the middle. Informative writing doesn't need a conclusion, and it really doesn't require any setting of the stage or introductory content. By contrast, a good evaluation starts with an opening component that identifies the subject of the evaluation, why it is relevant or important the reader, and the criteria by which the subject will be evaluated. The middle portion of the document presents all the detailed observations, sometimes in the form of a table or matrix. The last part of the structure is the conclusion, where we offer our opinion: Based on the evidence applied against the criteria, here's what I think.

You can find good examples of evaluative writing in *Consumer Reports*. If you were thinking about buying a DVD player or a refrigerator or snow tires, you could find articles there that evaluate the various models available. First, they define what they are discussing, why you as a reader might care about this kind of product, and what criteria are being used to evaluate the options. Next, they evaluate every model or brand point by point according to the criteria they listed. Usually this part is a combination of text containing anecdotal information about their testing and a table or matrix in which every brand or model is presented. Finally, they conclude the article by indicating which model is the "best buy" in their opinion. Do they care if you buy a DVD player or an icemaker or snow tires? No. It doesn't matter to them if you never buy anything. Their sole purpose is to take a look at what's available and offer an expert opinion about the various choices.

Writing to Persuade

With persuasion, we care very much about whether the reader is motivated to buy. Persuasion combines elements of information and evaluation. It should present facts accurately, and it should offer intelligent, informed opinions. But to be successful as persuasion, what we write or say should influence what the audience thinks, how they feel, or what they do.

Fortunately, the most effective pattern for persuasion, which I call the persuasive paradigm, is simple to understand and use. It consists of four steps.

First: State the Reader's Needs, Issues, Concerns   The initial

step in persuading someone is to demonstrate you understand the customer's needs, issues, or problem. Your first job is to summarize the business situation briefly, focusing on the gap to be closed or the competency to be acquired.

The vice president of sales for a large HVAC firm once asked me, "Why should I tell the customer what his problem is? He already knows that. If he didn't think he had a problem, he wouldn't have called us."

The answer, of course, is that we are not telling the customers something they don't already know. We're reducing their anxiety. They're worried that the solution we propose won't work because it's the right solution to the wrong problem. By showing customers that we "get" it, that we listened to them and understood what they told us, we raise their level of confidence. We help them feel confident that what we propose will be appropriate for them.

Second: Outcomes   Next, focus on the outcomes or results the customer wants to achieve. How will he or she measure success? What must the organization see in terms of results to make its investment in your products and services worthwhile?

This part of the persuasive paradigm is probably a bit counter-intuitive. After all, wouldn't it be more logical to state the problem and then give the solution? The thing to remember is that our goal is motivation. If we don't create a sense of urgency in the decision maker to go forward with our recommendation, we have not been successful in our persuasion effort. However, motivation does not come from problems and needs. Most businesses are faced with dozens and dozens of problems or needs, most of which will never get solved. Why? Because in the mind of the decision maker, "it's just not worth it." In other words, the return to be gained from fixing the problem doesn't outweigh its cost.

You don't want your solution to fall into the category of "not worth it." You create a sense of motivation in your customer by showing that the problem you are addressing is one that really should be fixed. The potential outcomes, the return on investment or improvement in productivity or whatever, are so big that he or she can't afford to wait. Focus on customers' pain to get their attention; focus on their gain to get their commitment.

Third: Recommend a Solution   Most proposals don't recommend anything. They lapse into informative writing and merely describe products or services in a flat, factual way. To be a solution, the products and services you are recommending must be linked to the customer's specific problem. "One of the problems you are facing is declining transaction value in your eCommerce transactions. The aspect of our recommendation that will help increase transaction value is. . . . "

Also, when you recommend a solution, sound like you believe in it. Say the words: "*We recommend* the immediate installation of LeadPoint asset management software." "*We urge you* . . . " "*We are confident* . . . " Don't be wishy-washy. Don't depend on telepathy to get your point across.

Fourth: Provide Evidence You Can Do It   If you're persuading in a sales situation, the last step in persuasion is to provide the evidence necessary to prove your company can do the job on time and on budget. Typical kinds of evidence that you might put in a proposal include references, testimonials, case studies, resumes of team members, project plans, guarantees, third-party validation such as awards, details about your management philosophy, your company history, and so on. It's vital in providing the evidence that you tie it back to the customer's needs and desired outcomes and that you emphasize your differentiators. This gives them a reason to say yes to you instead of a competitor.

Note that I am not saying your proposal should contain every one of these types of substantiation. Include only what the decision maker needs to see to feel confident about choosing you. That will be determined largely by the criteria that matter to this decision maker and by the specific requirements of the RFP, if there is one. Also, in a situation where you're responding to an RFP, your actual answers will be part of the evidence you provide—basically, evidence of your ability to comply with the customer's requirements and meet their objectives.

If your goal in persuasion is to motivate someone to do something or to change her attitude about something, the proof element really ties to her own self interest. Why should she bother? Is it really worthwhile? Is it the right thing to do?

The four steps of persuasion can be summarized as Needs, Outcomes, Solution, and Evidence. And these four words form the acronym NOSE. That's why many of my clients refer to the process of developing a persuasive message as doing a NOSE analysis.

CHAPTER 4

The Practice

Real-World Applications of the Language of Success

If you turned straight to this chapter, looking for a letter or memo to copy, I can't say I blame you. If you're facing an immediate writing task, especially if you're not sure how to begin, copying somebody else's document is pretty tempting. So if you find a good sample in this chapter of something you need to write, go for it!

But later, after the pressure is off, come back and take a look at this chapter more slowly. My goal is to show you how to implement the principles of the language of success. We've looked at why the languages of Fluff, Guff, Geek, and Weasel don't work and why you should banish them from your writing. We've considered how to make your messages clear, concise, correct, and appropriate to both your audience and your purpose. This chapter contains the practical examples that bring it all together.

Writing to Inform

In terms of sheer numbers, you'll probably write more messages to inform other people than any other kind. All of us do a lot of informing, even if our jobs are focused on evaluative writing (like an appraiser, for example) or persuasion (like a sales or marketing professional). We still need to give other people the facts they need to do their jobs, answer their questions, provide status updates, and so on.

As we discussed earlier, the basic structural pattern for presenting information is the funnel. Start with the most basic and important fact first. Then present the second most important fact. Then the third, and so on. This is the pattern that's used in newspapers and magazines and on news-oriented Web sites to present factual stories. Even a fledgling journalist knows to start an article with a short, focused lead that answers the reader's key questions: *Who? What? When? Where? How? Why?* Of course, the facts we present in answer to those questions will vary, depending on the audience.

One of my first consulting engagements was with a section manager at General Electric's Aircraft Engine Business Group, a brilliant man named Dr. Len Beitch. He led a team of nearly 200 PhDs in physics, chemistry, mathematics, engineering, and other complex disciplines, all looking at issues of safety and life management affecting GE's jet engines. Often they came up with important information affecting the design of engine components, the materials and manufacturing methods used to build them, or the economics of operation. And often the information they uncovered failed to have the impact Dr. Beitch knew it should have. That was where I came in. My job was to write the memos so that other people in the company understood them and could act on them correctly. But what we soon found was that a memo describing the results of fracture analysis in a new alloy would not work if we sent the same version to the Materials Lab and to the Executive Suite. Once we began to tailor the memos to suit the audience, understanding and impact soared.

So, as you prioritize your content, remember to ask yourself what your audience is most likely to think is important. Obviously, their opinion is the only one that matters, even if it's not the same as yours.

Simple Announcements
Here's an announcement of a new personnel appointment handled ineffectively:

Subject: Averaging UP!

I am pleased to announce that we continue to make progress on the commitment we made at the end of last year to add more valuable experience and build a stronger management team here at IntraModal Carriers. Although we already had a good team in place, every team can become better—even the New York Yankees or the San Antonio Spurs, right, Rob? So with that in mind, we're pleased to announce that once again we are averaging up with the addition of a strong talent to our line up, specifically the appointment of Sylvia Barones to be our new head of Alliance Marketing. Sylvia officially joins us on August 15, but many of you have already met her because she's been here in the offices off and on for the past two weeks, soaking up every bit of knowledge she can get her hands on. Sylvia will focus on helping our agents and brokers become more successful through innovative and cost-effective marketing programs. She has a great track record and produced outstanding results at her previous job with Rocky Mountain Railfreight. Let's all welcome her to the team and help her help us be more successful!

There are lots of things wrong with that memo. First, the subject line is worthless. It doesn't give you any useful information. Second, the memo itself is focused on what the writer cares about—some plan to improve the overall management team—rather than on what the vast majority of employees care about, namely, who is the new head of Alliance Marketing. Third, the style is chatty and breezy, with a false-sounding cheerfulness that sounds like Fluff. Fourth, it's filled with clichés, and the forced analogy between the employees of this transportation company and the Yankees or the Spurs is ridiculous. Fifth, it's hard to extract the key points because they're buried in a long, rambling paragraph. And finally, it contains generalities—"a great track record"—where specifics would be helpful, and specifics—"she's been here in the offices for the past two weeks"—where little or no information would be appropriate.

Here's the same announcement, written clearly and concisely and putting the important facts first:

Subject: Sylvia Barones named head of Alliance Marketing

Sylvia Barones has accepted our offer to become head of Alliance Marketing, effective August 15. Ms. Barones' responsibilities at IntraModal Carriers will include developing programs for our agents and brokers throughout North America.

She previously held a similar responsibility with Rocky Mountain Railfreight, where she helped grow indirect revenues over 300% in five years. We are excited to add her to our team. Please give her a warm InterModal welcome when you see her.

Here's another example. Would you classify it as successful or not?

Subject: Robbery May 24

I arrived at the store at about 8:30 a.m., unlocking the rear entrance as I usually do and turning on the lights. It wasn't until around 8:45 that I noticed the glass in the front display window shattered. Big shards of glass were everywhere, so it looked like somebody hit the window with a heavy object. For some reason the alarm did not go off when the glass was shattered, even though the night manager, Rajina Pickett, was certain that she had set the alarm.

When I saw the mess, I first called mall security and then called the police to report the damage. Next I started to look to see what had been stolen. By 9 a.m. the three clerks who were scheduled for that morning had arrived, so we systematically inventoried merchandise. First of all, the cash registers were not damaged as far as I could tell. However, we were missing a number of high-priced items, including three fur coats, more than a dozen watches, all of our necklaces and earrings, and numerous designer scarves. I estimate the total losses to be about $6,000.

The police took a full report and indicated they will be interviewing all of the store employees. They also took fingerprints from various locations around the store. The head of the investigation is Inspector Deborah McCall, who is in charge of robbery investigations for the

---

Brantley Police Department. Her direct number is 1-555-234-5678. She indicated she would get back to me within 24 hours with an update on the investigation.

In the meantime, the mall helped us cover the broken window and I have arranged to have the plate glass replaced tomorrow.

The preceding memo, which closely parallels one I actually saw at a major retailer, fails primarily because the store manager has written it chronologically. It fails to put the most important information first. Here's a revision:

Subject: Robbery at Store #179 on May 24

Store #179, Brantley Crossings Mall, was robbed during the night of May 24, between closing at 9:30 PM and opening at 8:30 AM.

An initial estimate of losses indicates approximately $6,000 worth of merchandise was taken. We lost no cash. There were no injuries. Property damage consists of a shattered storefront window. An itemized list of stolen merchandise is attached, although we may discover additional losses later.

Mall police and the local Brantley Police Department were notified immediately. The investigation is being handled by Inspector Deborah McCall (555-234-5678) of the Brantley P.D.

We opened for business by noon with the window boarded up. A new window will be installed tomorrow.

Giving Instructions

One of the most common forms of writing in a business or organizational setting is giving someone else instructions. The same principles apply to this kind of informational writing. To be successful, keep your sentences short, avoid jargon, and number each instruction separately. Here's an example of a government agency attempting to clarify for vendors how to deal with pre-existing partnership arrangements:

SUBJECT: TEAM POLICIES

The Government will recognize, the integrity and validity of contractor team arrangements; provided the arrangements are identified and company relationships are fully disclosed in an offer or, for arrangements entered into after submission of an offer, before the arrangement becomes effective. The government will not normally require or encourage the dissolution of contractor team arrangements.

The subject line is not very helpful, although that's probably the best part of this message. The first comma, which seems to have wandered in from some other sentence and decided to perch in this one like a bird on a telephone wire, actually makes the sentence much harder to understand. The use of big words (20 of the 55 words in this message have three syllables or more!) and the long first sentence (41 words long!) combine to make this thing unreadable. For some reason, "Government" is capitalized rather ominously in the first sentence, but is written "government" in the second one. Why? Notice, too, that the most important point doesn't even appear until the very end. And, when you get to the end, don't you find yourself wondering: *So what do they want me to do?*

Here's a rewrite:

SUBJECT: POLICIES AFFECTING SUBCONTRACTOR AGREEMENTS

Normally any pre-existing subcontractor relationships you have in place can stay in force after you win a new contract. This also applies to arrangements you make after you have submitted an offer but before the contract is awarded to you. However, we do need to know the details of all teaming arrangements. Please provide the following:

1. Name(s) of all subcontractors
2. Effective dates of the arrangement
3. Names of the key contact individuals for each company

Submit this information via e-mail directly to the designated Contracting Officer.

With this version, we not only understand the policy, we also know what to do. And we've managed to cut the readability score from a 16+ grade level equivalent (remember that 12 is the danger line and 10 is desirable) down to 10+.

Here's an e-mail that tries to give employees some simple instructions:

Subject: Warning

ALL,

As you may have read or heard about Microsoft released IE 7 a couple of days ago.

At this testing of IE 7 within Karlson's network environment and other applications is not complete. Accordingly, do not download IE 7 for use within the Karlson network.

If you believe you have a need for doing so, please contact me or Megan Chen via email to outline the need.

Sven

It's hard to take this message seriously. First, the salutation ("*ALL,*") sounds like we're being shouted at or scolded, immediately creating a negative impression. Avoid using all capital letters. It's unprofessional. Next, the opening sentence doesn't make sense. We can figure out what the writer is trying to say, but he definitely didn't say it. Third, the instructions need to be fleshed out a bit, I think. Here's how Sven could have handled his message more professionally and effectively:

Subject: Do not download IE 7 until testing is finished

Hi, everyone—

After months of marketing and advance discussion, Microsoft released its new web browser, IE 7, two days ago.

Unfortunately, new releases of software can sometimes create unexpected problems, ranging from security holes to incompatibilities with other applications to drains on network capacity. There's no reason to

---

continued

think that IE 7 will pose any problems, but we do need to test it thoroughly in our environment before anyone starts using it. At this point, our IT folks haven't finished the testing process. They expect to complete it within the next two weeks.

In the meantime, please do not download IE 7 to any computers that will connect to our corporate network. This includes your company-issued desktop and laptop computers and any systems you have at home that you use to dial in to our network.

If you believe you have a need for using IE 7 because of new functionality or for some other reason, please contact me or Megan Chen via email first. Briefly describe why you need it. We'll do our best to expedite the assessment for you.

Thanks for your help in keeping our operating environment stable and safe.

Sven

Answering Questions

When you answer a question, it's a good idea to reference the question itself. Your reader might be able to find the question in the chain of connected e-mails linked below your reply, but many e-mail systems automatically truncate the chain. Also, it's possible the person who asked the question has become so busy that he or she has now forgotten the context of the question. To make your answer easy to read and understand, use a subject line that references the fact that your reader asked you something and then restate the question in brief. After you do that, your answer will unfold naturally and logically. Here are two examples, one showing how not to do it and the other written in the language of success:

SUBJECT: Marketing

Gwen—

Lead generation from search engines, even those where we pay for top placement, has gone down over the past 18 months, so that it is now about equivalent to the number of leads generated from our print ads in specialist journals.

Reuben

Say what? Unless Gwen has had nothing to do for the past few days except to sit around waiting for your answer, she may find herself doing a double take at this message. The sentence is too long (41 words), but even worse is the fact that it seems to come flying at us out of nowhere. What is Reuben talking about? Why am I getting this m. . . . ? Oh, that's right. We asked him.

This e-mail would be clearer if we structured it differently:

SUBJECT: Your Q. about lead generation

Gwen—

You asked which method of generating leads was more productive for us now, search engines or print ads. The two sources are now almost identical. Over the past 18 months, the number of leads from search engines has declined, including those where we buy top placement. Leads generated by print ads have remained steady.

Please call me if you need more information.

Reuben
X 3713

Project Updates and Summaries

Project updates, project summaries, progress reports, status reports, and activity reports are all similar in that they provide readers with concise, accurate information about an ongoing body of work. This kind of report tells interested parties whether the work is on schedule, whether it has run into unexpected obstacles, whether it's still within budget, whether there are issues of "scope creep" that must be addressed, whether there have been any significant personnel changes, and so on. You might write a project update or similar report internally to keep your colleagues, particularly your boss, up to date on the status of your work. Even more common is the use of project updates and status reports to keep a customer informed about the status of work she is paying your company to handle.

Before you write the first update, think carefully about how you will format it, because each report in the series of updates should follow the same format. By using the same format for every report, you make it much easier for your readers to spot the specific information they want to know. You also simplify the reading process by repeating the organizational pattern. (This is similar to what happens when you write a series of clauses or bullet points in parallel structure. Once the reader sees the pattern is repeating, his or her task in comprehending your material becomes easier.)

What do your readers want to hear first? (In other words, in terms of the informative writing pattern, which bits of information in your project update or progress report have the broadest interest for your audience?) Chances are they want to hear (1) what specific tasks have been accomplished since the last report, (2) any challenges or problems that might affect schedules or budgets, and (3) next steps. Other areas of content that may be of high importance include the status of the budget, anything that affects staffing (vacations, illnesses, new hires, and so forth), and issues involving facilities, tools, or security.

Many project updates are wordy and hard to read because their authors organize them chronologically. They often start by rehashing the project, its purpose, past milestones, and similar information that isn't of primary relevance in any progress report except the very first one. Here's a sample progress report that starts slow and then gets lost in its own meanderings, ending with a disturbing projection of unexplained cost overruns:

SUBJECT: Miller Hall Energy Conservation Project Update

This project, as you all know, is focused on implementing a series of changes to Miller Hall on the south campus in order to reduce energy consumption. Miller Hall has long been one of the most important lecture halls on campus, particularly for the intro level core science classes, which can have as many as 500 students or more enrolled at once, a number which poses significant challenges for heating and cooling given the volume of "body heat" given off.

Anyway, since last month's report, we have made quite a bit of progress toward modifying electric consumption by changing the lighting scheme, mainly retrofitting with fluorescent lights. This work doesn't directly affect the comfort issues, at least in terms of room temperature and air flow, but as you may recall the original analysis indicated that more electricity was used for lighting than any other aspect of building operation. In fact, heating and cooling are third, behind the A/V plug load associated with the projectors and computers used in the lecture hall and in the second floor information lab.

During the coming month, we'll finish up the lighting modifications and complete installation of additional insulation in the exterior walls. The original cost estimates for the insulation proved to be too low, by the way. It looks like we're going to need an additional $10,750 to cover it.

If you have any questions, please feel free to give me call.

Later—

Ben Birchfield

We can improve this a lot by rewording the subject line to make it sound more like English, by using headings to separate out key content, and by putting the information in a reasonable order of importance:

SUBJECT: Update on the Energy Conservation Project for Miller Hall

This is the fifth monthly report on this project, as specified in our contract.

Work Completed: During the past month, we finished 85% of the lighting retrofits. This work included completely removing some fixtures and replacing all of the incandescent fixtures with fluorescents. All lights have been replaced except for six sconces located on the south portico.

Next Steps: During week one of the coming month, we will complete the lighting modifications. At the same time we will begin blowing insulation into the exterior walls.

continued

> **Key Concern:** Original estimates for the insulation were $10,750 lower than the actual costs will be. We project we will be able to save about half of that by resizing the air conditioning unit, but we still must address a probable budgetary shortfall of $5,000 to $6,000.
>
> **Staffing:** We have two open requisitions, but these open positions are not expected to affect the schedule significantly. Both will be filled by the end of the month.
>
> **Contact:** For questions or more details, call my mobile (555-987-1122).
>
> Ben Birchfield

Clarifying Information

If somebody writes and asks you to clarify a bit of information you previously provided, you might find yourself feeling a little irritated. Inherent in that request is a negative judgment about your skill in communicating. You might be tempted to point out that you communicated clearly the first time and that it was his or her haste or stupidity that created the confusion. Don't do that. Use a professional tone and keep your message on topic. Here are two versions of the same clarification. Which one would you rather receive? Which one would you feel better about writing?

> SUBJECT: Vacation Policy—2nd attempt!
>
> Lakisha—
>
> Just to be clear, I did NOT say that the new policy will replace personal days. We are attempting to give employees more flexibility in how they use vacation time and personal time, that's all. Nobody is taking anything away from you. You can use EITHER vacation OR personal days for any reason and you can even tack your personal days on to the end of your vacation. All you have to do is schedule your off time with your manager for anything that lasts more than one day.
>
> Hope that's clear now.
>
> Webb Neumann

We can improve this a lot by rewording the subject line to make it sound more like English by using headings to separate out key content and by putting the information in a reasonable order of importance. Oh, and we can drop the rude tone while we're at it.

SUBJECT: Clarifying the use of personal days and vacation time

Lakisha—

Thanks for writing.

I can see how the new policy might be a bit confusing, but the good news is that it's actually an improvement to what we used to do.

The intent of the new policy is to give each employee more control over how he or she uses both vacation time and personal days. As you know, each of us has three personal days a year. Traditionally, these have been for family matters, doctor visits, and so forth. Under the new policy, you can do anything you want with them. You can even add them on to the end of your vacation if you want. The only requirement, which is the same one we've always had, is that if you will be out of the office for more than one day, you need to schedule it with your manager.

Regards,

Webb Neumann

Writing to Evaluate

Everybody has an opinion. Unfortunately, not everybody's opinion is worth hearing. If you want your professional opinions to be heard, respected, and carefully considered, you need to communicate them in the language of success.

Writing an evaluation requires that you offer an opinion. The root meaning of the word "evaluate" is to form a critical opinion of something or someone, to determine its worth, scope, significance, or quality. If you are asked to evaluate two options for lunch, you probably won't feel much pressure. Nothing much hinges on your opinion. If you are asked to evaluate several options for sales management software, locations for a new retail outlet, choices for the theme of next year's marketing campaign, or candidates for an open position—well, the pressure on you to do the job right and communicate your opinion effectively will be much greater.

As a reminder, evaluations have their own structural pattern. They will be clearest and most effective when they follow a three-part format:

First: Provide your reader with a brief introduction in which you:
1. Identify the subject about which you are writing.
2. Indicate why your reader should be interested in your opinion.
3. Explain the criteria upon which you have based your judgment.

Second: Discuss the various options in terms of how they match up to the criteria of judgment you're using. You can do this by considering each option completely before discussing the next, or you can do it by stating your first criterion and then discussing all of the options in terms of it. (As a reminder, we discussed the comparison/contrast paragraph structure on pages 111 to 114, giving examples of the alternating and the block approaches.)

Third: State your opinion. Tell the reader, based on your evaluation of the options in light of the criteria, which is the best option.

The third step is the part of the process that makes many writers uncomfortable. It's the moment they may lose their courage and bail out of the process. But if you don't offer your opinion, you haven't done your job.

Comparison and Contrast

Comparing or contrasting is a common writing task where your opinions matter. Here's an example of a memo that compares and contrasts two branch offices:

SUBJECT: The Boston and Seattle Offices

Hi, Edward—

You asked for some information and insight into Boston and Seattle, the two offices where you'll be conducting your sales training. Each has its own personality, although I can't say whether that's related to the fact they're on opposite coasts or to the differences in their leadership and staff. Regardless, here are some facts about their size, team structure, and the general attitude you're likely to encounter in each location.

Boston

The Boston branch was the first office established outside our headquarters in New York. A total of about 150 salespeople work there, but your session will be attended by the top 25 performers. Your session will be held in their main conference room, which might be a tight fit.

Mitch Paxton is the head of the Boston office and he takes a keen interest in sales. He'll be attending your session, as will Terry Hoff, who is the head of business development for Boston and who reports to Mitch. The Boston office generally works on smaller projects than New York, and typically has a shorter sales cycle.

The team there likes to refer to themselves as "The Bostonians," and they tend to conduct business in a slightly more formal way. Mitch will want to start the meeting by introducing you and will be very clear about objectives. They also like to adhere to a definite schedule, with specific break times and punctuality. They can be a little slow to warm up, particularly to people from outside the company.

Seattle

The Seattle branch is similar to the Boston office in size, roles, and so forth. They are much more casual, both in their interactions and in their dress. You'll find they accept you quickly and, unlike most of the folks in Boston, the team in Seattle will be completely comfortable if you don't wear a suit and tie. By the way, they have a
continued

beautiful training facility in Seattle, which is provided by the building where the office is located. It's very nice and has rear projection
capabilities, electronic white boards, the whole works.

Cameron Greene is the head of the Seattle office. She will not be at
your session, however. Instead, her head of business development,
Tito Rodriguez, will be your host. Both of them have set goals around
improving sales in the office, particularly cross-selling of products,
so they're very excited about your workshop.

One thing I've noticed about the Seattle office is that they are quite re-
sistant to "group think." In other words, if they feel they're getting a
bunch of stuff that was cooked up in the head office, they're likely to
be skeptical or even dismissive. However, they're very receptive to
new ideas from outside. I'd recommend emphasizing your work with
other companies.

Logistics and Next Steps

My assistant, Ronni Piotrewski, has booked your hotel rooms and informed both offices of your requirements for A/V, chart paper, etc.

Edward, good luck with the session. I'm confident your program will
be well received in both offices and I know it can make a difference
for them.

Regards,

Andrea Trask

Definition and Classification

Sometimes different people within an organization or an industry
use the same words to mean very different things. Sometimes new
hires need to have basic terminology explained to them. And sometimes we need to organize what we have learned in the context of
what we already knew, relating facts and concepts within some general mental arrangement of categories. In all of these situations, we
will need to offer our opinions about the meaning of terms and about
the classification of knowledge. Here's an example:

COTS Products and Government Acquisition Standards

Introduction. Federal Acquisition Regulations have mandated that agencies select Commercial Off-the-Shelf (COTS) products whenever they are available. The assumption behind this regulation is that COTS products are likely to be less expensive, to be standardized in ways that reduce the costs associated with maintenance and upgrade, and to pose less risk since they are already in wide use. As a result, the whole subject of COTS products, their development and acquisition, has become important to companies who sell to the federal government and to those contracting officers who are making the selections. In particular, the question of what exactly constitutes a COTS product has become a topic of heated debate, since a company may find itself excluded from bidding processes if its primary products are not classified as COTS. Also, in certain areas of technology, particularly those associated with the Internet, with genetics, with nanotechnology, and several other areas, new technologies and new products emerge so fast that lists of approved COTS products in those fields rapidly become obsolete.

Defining characteristics. The characteristics that define a COTS product have not been consistently defined within the Federal Acquisition Regulations. In fact, in most cases bid documents do not define COTS at all. But from our experience and from a wide-ranging review of the literature, we have found that four characteristics are used most frequently. The first is **origin**. *Who developed the product? Is product development a core part of their business model? Do they have the infrastructure to continue product development in the future?* The second characteristic is **market acceptance**. *Who has bought this product or previous versions of it? How widely is it used?* The third characteristic is **ownership of the intellectual property** embedded in the product. *Has it been patented, copyrighted, trademarked, or otherwise protected?* The fourth is **sustainability**, which encompasses the issues of support, maintenance, and modifiability. *Is there a support structure in place to assist purchasers of this product? Can the product be modified easily? Does it already have interfaces or connections so that it works with other standard products? Is there a clearly defined plan for product development and evolution to minimize product obsolescence?*

General conclusions. It seems reasonable to conclude that a COTS product is one that has been developed by an organization that exists

continued

to create such products. Thus, neither a university research lab nor a consulting firm that does not otherwise market products is likely to produce a true COTS product. In fact, to have their products meet the first criterion of a COTS products, such organizations would need to partner with a firm that has a core competency in bringing products to market.

Second, a COTS product is one that has been purchased, installed, and used by other customers. The COTS product may include a claim of specific intellectual property rights, and the organization offering it will usually have a clearly defined program of support and maintenance. In the cases of software applications and technical equipment, the COTS products will also have issues of connectivity and integration already worked out.

In my opinion, because most of our product families are well recognized and in some cases are market leaders, we will not encounter any resistance to meeting the definition of a COTS product. However, for new products, particularly those that incorporate significant innovation, we should include content in our proposals and marketing literature that emphasizes the four criteria. In some cases, purchasing agents may reject the truly new product, even when that product is obviously superior, on the grounds that because it is new it doesn't meet the definition of a COTS product. This attitude is particularly common within the federal government where buying behavior tends to be risk averse. However, by focusing on the characteristics of origin, market acceptance (for related products or for our company's products as a whole), intellectual property, and sustainability, we can make a very good case that even a product that is being offered for the first time and that is based on a totally new paradigm can be classified as a COTS product.

Offering an Informed Opinion

Your role may require you to answer technical questions from a client or a colleague in which your opinion is the crux of the answer. Attorneys have to do this all the time. A client calls up and asks if establishing a self-directed trust will protect her assets from probate and preserve the value of her estate for her children. Accountants also have to write letters expressing their opinions. This is the heart of an audit report. Usually, what's important in an audit is not the actual numbers, but whether those numbers and the financial controls in place at the firm being audited pose any kind of concern. Physicians, financial advisors, architects, engineers, consultants—all of these professions, which involve mastery of a complex body of knowledge, will frequently require people to offer informed opinions.

Section 404 of the Sarbanes-Oxley Act requires auditors (and senior management) to report on whether a company has established adequate internal controls over its financial reporting. This is an instance in which failing to offer an expert opinion could lead to civil and criminal prosecution! For most of us, the stakes won't be that high, but we still need to use the structural pattern for effective evaluation so that our opinions will be clear, convincing, and easy to understand.

Here's an example in traditional letter format from a CPA. Besides using the basic format for an evaluation, I have also eliminated some of the typical jargon used by accountants in their reports. If you're an accountant, you might wince at what I've done here, because some of that language protects you legally from being held liable for your opinions. The problem with it, from the perspective of your clients, is that the same language that's protecting you is also clouding the meaning of your opinions. Because we're paying for your opinion, most of us think we have the right to actually understand it. That said, don't use this letter as a model until you talk with your senior partners and/or legal counsel. In other words, have them write an evaluation of it!

Mr. Marco Trezzini
Chief Executive Officer
Advanced Electric Manufacturing
Phoenix, Arizona

Dear Mr. Trezzini:

We have completed our audit of the financial statements of Advanced Electric Manufacturing for the fiscal year ending December 31, 2007, in accordance with auditing standards generally accepted in the United States of America. We examined the Company's internal control over financial reporting as an element of our auditing process so

continued

that we could offer our opinion on the Company's financial statements. However, we do not in this audit express an opinion on whether the Company's internal control is effective or adequate. To determine that, we would need to perform a complete review of the Company's operations and policies that was sufficient to identify all deficiencies in internal control that might be significant.

We did observe one matter that in our opinion is a control deficiency. Currently, the CFO's expenses are not reviewed by the Company's president or any other member of the senior management team. The president approves and signs checks to pay the CFO's expenses, but no one reviews the actual expense report. The potential for a misstatement of expenses from this practice is not significant. However, as a matter of consistency and improved control, we recommend that the CFO's expense report be reviewed and approved by a member of senior management before the reimbursement check is issued.

Sincerely,

Benton T. Knowles, CPA
Benjamin, Knowles and Levine, LLP

Competitive Analysis

How does your company stack up against your competition as a family-friendly place to work? How does a particular product you sell match up against others in the same space? Which nonprofit organization in your community is the most worthy recipient for funds from the Community Development Block Grant program? What kind of investment is safest for your elderly parents?

These are the kinds of questions a competitive analysis might answer. In writing the analysis, you need to use the same basic format for evaluative writing. Introduce your subject and indicate why it's important. Identify the criteria you're using as the basis for your analysis. Summarize your observations, perhaps in a chart. And then express your opinion.

Here's an e-mail written from a citizen's advisory board to members of a city council, analyzing how best to use the remaining $10,000 in block grant funding:

SUBJECT: Recommended use of remaining CDBG funds

Members of Council—

The following is an analysis of how to use the remaining $10,000 of Block Grant funds to benefit the community.

Criteria. As you know, in 2004 the City Council identified four funding areas as having the highest priority:

- Preventing homelessness and providing supportive services for the homeless
- Providing supportive health services, including mental health, for those without adequate resources
- Providing services for seniors and/or people with disabilities
- Providing supportive services for families and/or youth

In addition, Council guidelines established in 2006 for the use of CDBG funds indicate that special consideration should be given to programs that primarily serve residents of the City.

The candidate programs. With these factors in mind, we have reviewed applications from two candidate agencies: The Literacy Project and The Caring Hearts Hospice of Jackson County. We have scored each program, using a "0" if it does not address the criterion, a "1" if it partially or indirectly addresses it, and a "2" if the criterion is part of its core mission.

	The Literacy Project	Hospice
Prevention of homelessness	1	0
Supportive health services	0	2
Services for seniors and/or those with disabilities	1	1
Services for families and/or youth	1	1
Total	3	4

continued

Both programs offer services on a countywide basis. Approximately 45% of the clients served by the Literacy Project are City residents. For Hospice, the number is slightly lower, approximately 40%. However, the number of people served in total by Hospice is much larger. Last year, Hospice provided services to 4,320 terminally ill and bereaved clients. Thus, over 1,700 City residents received support from Hospice. By contrast, the Literacy Project served 930 clients, of which 419 are residents of the City.

Conclusion: Although both programs are clearly worthwhile and deliver significant value to the City, we recommend allocating the funding to Hospice. Based on the key criteria, Hospice is slightly more in line with the guidelines established by Council. In addition, it serves more people in the City.

Respectfully submitted,

Citizens Advisory Board

Here's a competitive analysis written to help a couple nearing retirement reallocate their investments so that they will have sufficient income once they have stopped working. In this case, the financial advisor who is writing the evaluation doesn't particularly care which option the couple chooses. (If the advisor did care, he or she would be writing a persuasive message and that would require a different structural pattern entirely.)

SUBJECT: Options for investing your retirement funds

Dear Ted and Doris—

It was great to see you yesterday! And how exciting to hear that you're about ready to retire. Ted, I'm sure the trout from here to Montana are all feeling very nervous if they've heard that you'll soon be pursuing them full time!

You asked my opinion about what to do with some of your investment accounts to make sure you have plenty to live on going forward. As we discussed, the most important factor for you is the security of your principal. You do not want to take any risks with this money, since it's your "nest egg" for the next phase of your life. Liquidity is also an issue, because you want to have access to your money in case you encounter unexpected large bills. However, we agreed that if you can convert your investment into cash in a few weeks without incurring too much of a penalty, your liquidity requirements will be met. Finally, as you both correctly indicated during our conversation, generating a high return from your investments is a low priority now. That's something the young folks need to worry about. You've already accumulated what you need. Now it's just a matter of using it wisely.

Options. We discussed three kinds of financial vehicles that will meet your objectives. There are lots of different "brands" to choose from for each of the three, but first you need to choose which type of investment vehicle best meets your objectives.

The first option is a **certificate of deposit.** These are very low risk investments. Your principal is secure with a certificate of deposit (or CD), you will not lose any of your principal no matter what happens in the economy, and you will earn a reasonable rate of return. However, a CD is not a truly liquid investment. Your money is not as readily available if you need it before the term of the certificate expires. Usually you can get it, but you'll pay a sizable penalty.

The second option is a **mutual fund.** A mutual fund is an investment in which your money is put into several different, smaller investments of the same type. You indicated you already own some mutual funds that invested in stocks, which is a fairly common type. Generally speaking, mutual funds are riskier than certificates of deposit, if only because the stock and bond markets are riskier. As a result, you could lose a lot of your principal. The money is more liquid, however. You could liquidate a mutual fund and have cash transferred into your checking account in a matter of a couple of days.

The third option is an **annuity.** Many retirees like annuities, particularly fixed annuities, because they offer a guaranteed check each month. Liquidity is not much better with these than with a certificate

continued

of deposit, however, and in a period of rapid inflation an annuity may not keep pace.

My recommendation: In my opinion, all of these are good options and any of them can meet your retirement needs. However, given the size of your retirement funds and your focus on preserving principal, I favor either the CD or the annuity.

When you two get back from Katie's wedding, please give me a call and we can look at some specific programs in those categories. In the meantime, have a great trip!

Best regards,

Chet Tillinghurst

You can probably see that this memo is oriented more toward explaining the differences among the types of investments without taking a strong stand. In this case, the writer is simply trying to play the role of trusted advisor and give his clients clear, relevant information in a jargon-free message so that they understand their choices. His opinions are found in statements like "mutual funds are riskier than certificates of deposit" and "liquidity is not much better." Somebody who was trying to sell Ted and Doris one of those products might want to argue those assertions with him. But the tone in his message is even-handed and direct, and he is placing the responsibility on his clients either to make the decision themselves or to ask him for additional information and more specific opinions.

Performance Appraisals

Few documents cause more angst among managers than performance appraisals. Like many of the other evaluative documents we have discussed, writing a performance appraisal can feel risky— *What if the employee gets mad? What if he sues?*—and may require a good deal of finesse to handle effectively. Telling someone his or her job performance is poor is about as appealing as telling someone her newborn baby is ugly. Any volunteers for that assignment?

Well, whether it's a fun job or not, performance appraisals are important. They provide concrete guidance for employees who want to improve. They provide documentation to justify specific personnel actions—salary increases, promotions, even terminations. They are useful in keeping both employees and managers aware of the company's direction and key objectives.

If you work for a larger company, one that has an HR department, your firm probably has a standardized process for handling performance appraisals, including forms, a rating system, and guidelines on appropriate and inappropriate ways to handle the appraisal. They might even provide you with software that will generate the appraisal document automatically. Normally, though, you will need to write up your opinions and any next steps as an evaluation report.

Most smaller organizations won't have much formal structure in place to guide you in handling performance reviews. You'll need to do the best you can to be consistent, fair, and clear in providing feedback to employees. Usually you will start with the person's job description as the basis for generating your key evaluative criteria. What are the primary responsibilities this person is supposed to handle? What specific tasks has he or she been given? How well has he or she performed against standardized metrics—for example, how well has a salesperson done against the assigned quota? What you say about a given employee and what kind of rating system you use will be up to you, but the way you say it should be based on the general format for writing to evaluate. (Bear in mind that what you say in a performance review can have serious legal ramifications. I'm not even pretending to tell you how to handle those issues; I'm just showing you how to put your thoughts together in a way that's effective for you and the employee. If you're concerned about possible legal issues with an employee review, talk to your in-house attorney, your HR department, or at least get a good book on the subject.)

Before you conduct a performance review, notify the employee who will be reviewed in writing several weeks beforehand. This will give the employee time to gather notes and material that he or she thinks will be relevant for the interview. In your e-mail notifying the employee of the interview, identify the subjects and areas of performance you plan to discuss, including training needs, career growth, or other topics. However, make sure you don't start the evaluation process in the announcement by indicating "problems" or areas of "poor performance" that you want to discuss. Keep the invitation factual and objective: just the time, place, location, duration, and topics. Use the informative format to set the interview up.

Some managers like to have the entire appraisal written up in advance of the "interview." They go through it with the employee and then shove it across the desk for the employee to sign. That's not an interview process, and it's likely to kill the employee's sense that the process is open and that his or her manager is willing to listen. You'll get better results if you have an agenda for the interview, including specific questions, incidents, accomplishments, and other areas for discussion, and then write the appraisal afterwards, based on the conversation you have. You may not change your mind about the employee's ranking, but the process will feel more collaborative and a little less threatening.

When it comes time to write up your review, include the following elements:

- Employee's name and contact information
- Job title and, if appropriate, job classification and/or salary grade
- Description of the job, including key responsibilities
- Specific job-related criteria that will be used in evaluating the employee's job performance
- Specific, detailed comments about the employee's performance in the context of the criteria—focusing on whether the employee exceeded, met, or fell short of expectations the organization has for someone in this role
  - You can compare the employee's performance with the objectives you set with him or her at the last performance appraisal
  - You can cite critical incidents of positive or negative performance, specific examples of work accomplished, or significant personal events that had a positive or negative impact on the employee's performance
- Any specific tasks, assignments, special roles, or other elements of the person's job that transcend the usual job responsibilities, plus comments on how the employee performed in handling them
- An overall performance rating
- Areas of particular strength

- Areas where the employee would like to develop additional skill and/or areas where the manager thinks additional training or skill development would benefit the employee or company
- Action steps for the employee and/or the organization, how they will be measured, and a timeline for completion

Acknowledge the fact that the process is subjective. That's not a defect. A defect would arise if the person whose subjective opinion forms the basis of the appraisal (that would be you, the boss) is not qualified by experience or training to have a sound opinion. A defect would arise if the manager doing the appraisal were unable to write it up clearly and concisely.

Here's an example of a performance appraisal. It's for a truly outstanding employee who had a great year, but it illustrates the basic principles.

**Pointillism Corporation
Performance Review
for
Antoine Leboque**

Employee Name: Antoine Leboque
Date of Review: June 1, 2007
Next Review Date: May 29, 2008
Hire Date: May 30, 2003

Position: Director of Marketing and Channel Development
The Director of Marketing and Channel Development is responsible for promoting the company and its products, generating leads that result in closed sales, supporting the direct sales team and the reseller community with effective materials, designing and maintaining the corporate Web site, handling news releases and public relations activities, investigating and recommending innovative ways to leverage technology to achieve marketing goals, and other duties as assigned.

Overview:
Antoine, it has been another successful year for you. As your supervisor, I am proud to be working with you. You are a professional and

continued

---

a smart business person. Your energy is amazing. You have continued to grow and change even when you are burdened all day with getting specific projects done. In fact, I was amazed at the amount of work you completed this year when I went back to see what you actually did. Here are just a few of your accomplishments:

Accomplishments since your last review

- You attended an e-marketing seminar and it really fired you up. You came back with lots of new ideas that you have implemented over the past six months.
- You successfully coordinated four trade shows, plus regional training sessions with our resellers.
- You secured five keynote speaking engagements at national conferences for our CEO.
- You increased the volume and quality of communication between marketing and the rest of the company by issuing more frequent e-mails on marketing's achievements.
- You put into place a plan and a system to track all of the sales from our resellers.
- You continue to contribute to company morale through coordinating events like the baseball game, casino trip, Bastille Day party, etc.
- You have implemented improved statistical reporting. As a result, we have more accurate stats on web visits, leads, first presentations, closed sales, etc.
- You wrote and placed articles and press releases that have driven activity to our Web site.
- You created a new technical handout that will help in web sales and will support our inside sales team.
- You segregated customer lists by vertical market and type, helping us recognize trends in the marketplace and make intelligent choices about marketing activities.
- One of your best achievements this year was to organize for your department what happens, daily, weekly, monthly, and quarterly. It provides clear direction on what needs to be accomplished. It also shows the rest of the company what you do and why.
- You have continued to assist the president in completing the Board Meeting presentations and statistics.
- You coordinated a superb and successful Reseller Community Kick-off in January.

- You coordinated the data gathering and writing of seven new case studies for our library of proposal content.
- You developed our first series of Webinars, which were a wonderful addition to the company's marketing plan.

Comments from Other Employees

I solicited feedback from other employees about your job performance and received the following comments:

- *Antoine has been very helpful and supportive each time I have called. The support materials his group has put together have been great—the sales manual, resource disk, etc. I really appreciate him being on the team.*
- *I'm still in awe of his dedication and enthusiasm. He has drive, that's for sure.*
- *I can only say that he consistently amazes me with his new ideas, what he's able to get done, and how willing he is to pick up the ball on just about anything.*

Places to Grow, Talents to Develop

- Proactively presenting ideas for roll-outs, products, etc. You tend to wait to design the roll-out program for new releases and new products until the development is near completion. As a result, the roll-out isn't as strong as we would like it to be. Please develop some specific suggestions on how we can improve this area.
- You are remarkable in generating many excellent ideas. You are not always as successful at executing those ideas. For example, during the past year you recommended a postcard campaign using the cartoon character, a Web-based training library for users to access, and getting the CEO booked on business TV programs. These are all great ideas, but none of them were completed. Let's work on creating an activities list, delegating tasks as appropriate, and staying to a timeline so that your great ideas aren't wasted.
- As always, you need to look for ways to generate more leads and more awareness for the company for the least amount of money. This will involve monitoring the industry for creative ideas we can adapt and being on the alert for new programs we can try.

continued

Uncompleted from Last Year's Goals
- Develop a plan for international growth in the next year.

What do we want to achieve for the next year?
- We need change. It is time to change the message, shake up our standard notion of who we sell to, our pricing models, anything that we take for granted. But the change must be focused on generating quick growth in net revenue and/or market share. Your key assignment will be to develop a new marketing plan for the second half of this year to be implemented in 2008.
- Increase the percentage of people who come to our site and buy from 2% to 3.5%.
- Keep accurate and timely competitive information and share it frequently with the sales force.
- Track results from the Web presentations program, particularly in terms of qualified leads and closed sales.
- Start participating at the Board Meetings, making formal presentations to the Board of Directors and being part of the decision team.

Ranking and Recommendation
- Antoine Leboque is an outstanding employee. Top ranking.
- Recommendation: promotion effective immediately to Vice President, Marketing.

Comments:

Signed:_____(Antoine Leboque)

Date: _____

Writing to Motivate

You might be wondering why we have a section of documents focused on motivating others, when we only have three controlling purposes for business writing—informing, evaluating, and persuading. You may also be surprised to see that I've included documents that instruct or train within the subcategory of motivation. Shouldn't instructing and training be part of informing?

The answers are, first, motivation is a subset of persuasion and, second, unless they are motivated, adult learners will blow off any instructions or training they get. Think about the broad definition of persuasion: It's a type of communication that has as its primary goal influencing the audience by changing what they think, how they feel about something, or what they do. In terms of that definition, it's clear that motivation is a form of persuasion. The key difference is that persuasion is usually focused on action as an ultimate goal—the client signs the contract, senior management adopts our plan. Motivation is successful when the message changes the recipient's feelings or attitude or enables him or her to see things in a different way.

Motivation is usually less transactional than persuasion. People still need a reason to change their attitude or their thinking, and the reason is likely to be related to their own needs or values. But we often can't resort to the typical promises we use in a sales or marketing message, such as increased revenue, greater productivity, or some other bottom-line measure of results. Instead, we may need to appeal to psychological values—being a team player, behaving in a logical manner, acting ethically, or perhaps growing as a person.

Maslow's hierarchy of needs starts with the basic human needs for survival (air, water, food, shelter) and moves upward through connectedness with others, esteem and respect, and ultimately what Maslow called "self-actualization." Often writers appeal to their audience's desire to meet these needs as the foundation for a motivational message. In the military, troops are likely to be motivated to withstand the risks of combat and to put aside their own basic need for physical safety through an appeal to needs that transcend personal survival—relatedness to others, for example, or the approval and respect of others, particularly loved ones, trusted leaders, or the individual's concept of God.

For most of us, fortunately, motivating others isn't a matter of life and death as it is in the military. We're trying to motivate our colleagues, subordinates, subcontractors, investors, and others so that they'll work harder, stay enthusiastic, accept a new direction, or just be patient. Some of the most interesting research into motivating others in a work setting was done by Frederick Hertzberg, who found that the things that motivated people at work were unrelated to the things that made them dissatisfied. The key motivators were the opportunity for achievement, significant recognition for success, the pleasure involved in doing the work itself, the opportunity to exercise greater responsibility, and the opportunity for advancement. The things that are most likely to make people unhappy include company policies, bureaucratic behavior, weak or inept supervision, perceived salary discrepancies, difficult relationships with other people, and the working conditions themselves. Removing a source of dissatisfaction does not result in higher motivation to work harder. What this suggests is that if you wanted to motivate employees to fully embrace a new safety policy, you'd have better success if you created contests and gave out prizes for success than if you simply remind them that working conditions will be better if they follow the new safety guidelines. Cash bonuses could also work. But just because you have attached cash bonuses to get everyone fired up about adhering to the new safety procedures doesn't mean you will also do away with grumbling about salaries (they will perceive the bonuses as being separate from salaries and will argue that their salaries should be adjusted regardless of any bonus program). Likewise, motivating employees to apply the new safety procedures in order to get rewarded doesn't mean they won't still complain about having a bunch of new policies to follow.

Another challenge in motivating others is to overcome their suspicion that we are acting in our own interests. It's difficult for employees to trust management even in the best-run companies, because senior management is seen to be very different from ordinary employees. This sense of difference creates what is called in psychological jargon "cognitive dissonance." When we hear our manager telling us to do one thing—work longer hours—but we are getting messages from our peers, our friends, or our family that we shouldn't be a sucker, that we should spend more time on our lives outside of work, we will experience a mental discomfort from the tension between these two points of view. Whom do we trust? Our tendency is to trust those who seem to be most like us and who seem to have our interests in mind. The kind of authoritarian and callous messages we saw in the first section of this book, written by two CEOs who wanted to rally their troops, only serve to increase our tension and reduce our motivation to work harder. To be successful in motivating others, we must try to focus first on meeting a fundamental need that they think matters, solving a problem that is distracting or bothering them, and then turn attention to helping them reach their goals. If they agree with our analysis of the situation—*that is a problem I'd like to see solved; that is a goal I'd like to see achieved*—then they are more likely to be motivated to do what we want.

On the following pages are some short examples of motivating others, ranging from very simple to rather complex. The underlying pattern in each case remains the fundamental pattern of persuasion: needs (the reader's need, not ours), outcomes (achieving a goal or addressing a value they support), solutions (in this case, the solution is for them to respond in a certain way), and evidence (details or proof that we will keep our part of the bargain).

Making a Request

One of the most common reasons we write e-mails is to ask questions or request help from someone else. When we ask someone to do something for us, we need to provide a little bit of motivation for them to want to do it. Suppose you just wrote:

Subject: Adapting to Unix

Luka—

Can you describe how we adapt our system to run in a Unix environment? I need 250 words on that by next Friday. Thnx.

Madeline

There are a lot of things wrong with that message, from the lousy subject line all the way to the text-messagy spelling of "Thanks," but the biggest problem is that there's a good chance Luka will ignore us. Why should he bother to respond to this rather rude request? However, if we provide a bit of context and act politely, we are probably providing all the motivation a well-meaning colleague needs to respond to us:

Subject: Need your help to win the Consortium bid

Hi, Luka—

Can you give me about 250 words on how we go about adapting our system to run in a Unix environment? I need it for the big university consortium RFP we're responding to. I think the cross-platform functionality we offer will be a huge differentiator for us.

Can you get it to me by the end of next week, please? Thanks!

Madeline

Madeline can assume that Luka understands how important the big opportunity with the university consortium is to the company as a whole. He probably wants to be part of a successful effort. As a team player, he also understands that his contribution will help the company, perhaps leading to recognition for the contributors and financial rewards for the firm as a whole. Finally, Luka probably enjoys talking and writing about this topic, assuming it's his chosen area of specialization. These are all adequate motivators in a healthy organization. (Unfortunately, there are work environments where colleagues see no reason to help each other. "That's not my job," the subject matter experts growl when asked to contribute to a proposal. Obviously, that's a dysfunctional organization, one that has problems that go far beyond the way employees write memos and e-mails to each other.)

If you are asking for help from someone outside your organization, particularly a stranger or someone you know only slightly, you need to give more thought to motivating him or her to respond. Why should he bother? What have you done already that makes your appeal to her a reasonable step at this point? How will she benefit? How much work are you asking for and how easy will it be for him to respond? Here's an example:

Dear Dr. Sebastian—

Your books on the creation and management of virtual teams, particularly the use of technology to facilitate collaboration, have been extremely valuable to us. However, we are looking for the answer to what we think is an important question, and so far we can't find anything. I've read both of your books and have tried a number of Web-based searches for the answer to an important question, but so far I've come up empty.

As you have pointed out, virtual teams pose unique challenges, including how best to do performance appraisals. Our question is: Do you think it's better to use 360 evaluations for the members of a virtual team, or should we stick with traditional methods of appraisal?

By the way, we are the first state agency in Georgia to move to a virtual work environment. We've seen the savings you predicted in your first book, particularly from having less capital tied up in office space in our regional locations. We've also seen an overall increase in worker productivity. We're just struggling to define the best methods, HR tools and processes for this new environment.

Thank you very much for any ideas you're willing to share. You can reply to this e-mail or, if it's more convenient, you can call me at the number below.

Regards,

Gaylord J. Blount, Executive Director

Instructing

Giving someone instructions or teaching him or her how to perform a task more efficiently may seem like a clear instance of writing to inform. But as I said earlier, if you don't motivate the audience to do the task the way you're teaching them to, they'll lapse back into old, comfortable habits.

Adults can be challenging students. Unlike children, adults must choose to learn. We don't give children that option. Learning is pretty much the core of their job description for the first 18 to 25 years of their life. Once they're in the world of work, however, they may decide their learning phase is over, and they will choose to pay attention only if your instructions are linked to their ability to achieve important personal goals. That's our first clue on how to motivate adults to learn: We must link the learning process to something they care about.

Other keys to success include connecting what we're teaching them to what they already know, either from prior training or from experience. We need to demonstrate that the instructions we're providing are relevant to their work (or some other aspect of their life that will make knowing these things valuable). They need to see that what we're covering is practical and useful, and we must address them in a respectful tone.

In trying to teach and motivate people how to do a work task differently, we need to overcome a lot of demotivating factors. Most people are afraid of failing, particularly in front of others. Some of them are afraid of change, thinking that if their work changes they may not be able to function as successfully as they have in the past. They may have had a very negative experience in a similar situation in the past, where the instructions weren't clear or didn't produce the promised results or made the job more difficult. It's better to address these kinds of concerns explicitly before you try to provide your instructions, rather than ignoring them and hoping they won't be a factor.

One way to make your instructions clearer and more vivid is to present them by means of a controlling metaphor or analogy. Try to choose an analogy that will be understandable to everyone who is getting your message. Using an analogy from American football to an international group of workers may fail, because (a) most of the recipients think "football" means soccer, and (b) none of them understand what on earth you're talking about when you say "sometimes a great tight end is going across the middle and sometimes he is blocking." (In fact, one can only speculate what imagery such phrasing as "a great tight end" or "going across the middle" would bring to the minds of employees in Europe and Asia.)

Here's an e-mail designed to train employees on the process of creating an archive file for old e-mail messages and to motivate them to start using it to get old files off the server:

Subject: Steps to avoid e-mail server shut down

Everyone,

Yesterday, as you all know by now, our e-mail server crashed, cutting us off from each other and from the outside world. That's simply not acceptable to any of us.

Why did it happen? The server is overloaded because many e-mail accounts contain hundreds of MBs of content that could be deleted or moved.

In order to prevent the problems we suffered yesterday from happening again, each of us needs to create an Archive file (.pst file) and move as much as we can off the Exchange server. You will still be able to open and read the information in the Archive files. You're not losing access to information that you need or might need in the future. You're just putting it in storage. An analogy might be what people do when they rent a self-storage locker to keep furniture and other belongings that they no longer have room for in their house.

To create your own "self-storage locker" for old e-mails, set a reasonable limit for what you want to keep on the Exchange server. Ed and I recommend only keeping the last 90 days in your Inbox and Sent folders, and no more than a year's worth of messages in any other folder.

It would be best if you create your Archive file on your own workstation. If you want to create a backup, you can also put a copy of your Archive file on a network server other than the one we use for Exchange. The server named Goliath has plenty of open space. Call me if you need instructions on how to move a copy of your Archive file to Goliath.

To create a new file and move or copy items to it, follow these steps:

1. On the **File** menu, point to **New**, and then click **Outlook Data File**.
2. To create a Microsoft Outlook Personal Folders file (.pst), click **OK**.
3. In the **File name** box, type a name for the file, and then click **OK**.
4. In the **Name** box, type a display name for the .pst folder.
5. Select any other options you want, and then click **OK**.

continued

When you create your .pst file, you can add a password of up to 15 characters. Remember our guidelines about using "strong" passwords that combine upper- and lowercase letters, numbers, and symbols. (Weak passwords don't mix these elements. A strong password: Y6dh!et5. A weak password: House27.) Create a strong password that you can remember so you don't have to write it down.

If you select the **Save this Password** in your password list check box, make a note of the password in case you need to open the .pst from another computer. Select this check box only if your Microsoft Windows user account is password-protected and no one else has access to your computer account.

The name of the folder associated with the data file will appear in the Folder List. By default, the folder is called Personal Folders.

Drag any item from your current folders to the new folder. Press CTRL while dragging to copy items instead of moving them.

We need to move over 250 gigabytes of data off the Exchange server, so please create your Archive file soon. If you have any questions about the instructions I've provided or anything else related to your Archive file, please e-mail me or call me at extension 2178.

Thanks for your cooperation! Nobody wants e-mail to go down again, and the budget simply does not have room for additional servers at this point.

Regards,

Alec Winters

Reprimanding

Reprimanding an employee is best handled by doing it in person as soon as possible after the mistake was made. Occasionally, you might need to follow up in writing, particularly if you need to document the incident and your response to it for the employee's file.

The goal of reprimanding someone for poor performance or a serious mistake in behavior is to motivate him to change his ways.

Unless you're just going through the motions of reprimanding the employee and your actual purpose is to create a paper trail so you can justify firing the person, you will want to handle a reprimand tactfully and focus on ways to motivate him to do better in the future.

To get the employee's buy-in to a reprimand, which is likely to be a scary and humiliating experience, don't dwell on what he or she did that was unacceptable. Identify it clearly, but then move on to discuss what it will take to prevent the problem from occurring again. Assume that the person wants to do a good job. Avoid any language that shames or blames the person. And definitely avoid any language that might be actionable, including terms such as *lazy, rude, stupid, incompetent,* and so on. Assume the employee has positive intentions regarding work generally and this incident specifically. You probably solicited ideas on how to prevent the problem from reoccurring when you discussed the problem with him or her in person. Mention the employee's suggestions in your summarizing message. Finally, if your goal truly is to motivate the employee, avoid using fear tactics such as threats of termination or other punitive measures. That's particularly important if you are dealing with an isolated incident.

Here's an example of a reprimand directed at an otherwise good employee:

Subject: RE: Your use of e-mail at work

Peter,

I just want to follow up on our conversation from yesterday, August 3. As we discussed, corporate policy prohibits any employee from using our e-mail system for any purpose not directly related to his or her work responsibilities.

Over the past few weeks, you have sent e-mails to your friends and family members and have used the corporate e-mail system to place orders on various Web sites. All of these actions fall into the prohibited category.

You indicated that you were unaware of the corporate policy and that now that you clearly understand it, you will adhere to it in the future.

continued

Knowing you as I do, I'm confident that will be the case. Restricting your e-mails to other employees at Dunkmeister and Brown, our clients, our prospects, and our vendors will solve the problem completely.

You suggested installing an open terminal in the lunchroom where employees could check their personal e-mail, surf the Internet, place orders, and so forth during lunch and during breaks. That idea has a lot of merit. I'll bring it up at the manager's conference in two weeks and will also check with IT about what that would require from a technical standpoint.

Please call on me if you have questions about following this policy or any others in the future.

Regards,

Buck Mueller

Communicating with Employees: Morale

When times are tough, employee morale can droop. Your job as a leader is to communicate with employees in a clear, direct way so they feel motivated to continue working hard. Using a metaphor or a story can be effective in engaging the audience's emotions. Great coaches, teachers, and military commanders understand the power of a vivid story to raise spirits and motivate top performance.

As we already discussed, motivating others also requires delivering a message that is in alignment with their values. That might mean making an appeal linked to their belief in God, to their concern or commitment to their family, to their patriotism, or to their fears. However, in most business settings, these are not appropriate ways to generate motivation. Instead, your message might appeal to the readers' logic, reason, or sense of fairness. You might appeal to satisfying their ego needs to be a winner, gain recognition, get more responsibility, or be seen as a leader. Or you could play upon their desire to achieve or display excellence in their work life. Sometimes a motivational message aimed at improving morale can be based on the shared desire among all employees to remove an unpleasant or dangerous situation.

Some managers realize that at times you can motivate employees by tapping into dysfunctional behaviors and attitudes. Most people have some emotional baggage, and many of us hear tapes playing in our head where mommy or daddy is telling us we need to be better, we need to try harder, we need to hurry up, or we need to stop sniveling and be tough. Tapping into these dysfunctional motivations is extremely risky. You may get what you want in the short term, but you may also trigger behaviors in the co-dependent employee that have profoundly negative consequences.

Here's an example of a message sent by an HR manager, trying to address disappointment and anger among employees over changes to the company's healthcare benefits. It combines an appeal to logic with an appeal to removing a dangerous situation in an effort to improve employees' attitudes toward the new benefit offering.

Subject: Your concerns about the new healthcare plan

Fellow employees,

Last month we announced a change in our healthcare provider and a restructuring of the healthcare benefits. I have received many questions and comments about the change, and many of you have expressed concern that the new plan has a higher co-pay and a slightly higher monthly premium than our old plan.

Both facts are true, but we are very optimistic that in the long run the new plan will save us a lot of money so that employee contributions can go down and the co-pay can be adjusted downward as well. Let me explain why and what you can do to make it happen.

The old plan
The difference in our new plan compared to our old one is that the old one was traditional healthcare insurance provided by an outside company, while our new plan is a self-insured model. Under the old plan, our insurance carrier took a snapshot of our employees and their state of health, then used its experience to set our premiums. At the end of the year, if all of us did a good job of staying healthy and staying out of the medical system, it didn't do us any good. The premiums stayed
continued

in the insurance company's pocket. Over the past few years, premiums have escalated much faster than the rate of inflation—in fact, faster than the rate of almost anything else in the economy. To stay competitive against overseas manufacturers, we have to keep total operating costs down. But we are committed to doing it in a responsible, fair way.

The new plan

Under our new plan, we are paying doctors, hospitals, and other care givers directly. Our insurance provider only starts to pay if our costs are much higher than expected. Then they kick in to prevent us from incurring a major financial loss. What this means is that the premiums we are putting toward healthcare coverage stay with us **if we don't use them.** The healthier we are, the less we pay, both as individuals and as a company.

Wellness as a way of life

One important difference between our old plan and the new one, besides the self-insurance aspect, is the new focus on wellness. Staying healthy will have a bottom-line impact on us and our company. As a result, we are investing heavily in promoting healthy lifestyles. We will sponsor smoking cessation workshops; stress reduction programs; and active management of chronic conditions, including diabetes, obesity, asthma, and many more. The result will be fewer health-related problems, lower total costs, and a much higher quality of life for most of us.

I know that providing quality healthcare coverage for your family matters to you. But I want you to know that it matters to all of us, because we are all members of the Atkinson Wire family. Please give the new program a chance to work. Please participate in any and all activities that will promote wellness. And please share with me any ideas you may have about improving our healthcare benefit while keeping a lid on costs.

Please call on me if you have questions about following this policy or any others in the future.

Best wishes for healthy living (so we can all enjoy reduced costs),

Sarah Feinstein
Director of Employee Benefits

Communicating with Suppliers: Responsiveness

Every business depends on vendors and suppliers to provide goods and services. Motivating those outsiders to give us their best quality materials and effort can be a tough challenge. If you represent a major account, they're likely to be responsive. But if you're not a huge account or if they've had your business for many years, they may take the relationship for granted.

If that happens, you may need to deliver a clear message that motivates the vendor to get back on track.

May 19, 20XX
Xavier Winkler
Tuscan Tile
7391 Willow St.
Glendale, AZ

Dear Xavier,

Over the past few years, we have had the opportunity to work on some great projects together. As the general contractor, we were very proud of the tile work you did on the new City Hall building, and we think you handled your part of the contract to retrofit county park restrooms for ADA compliance in a timely and cost-effective way.

Unfortunately, our current contract on the new headquarters for the Imbroglio Systems corporate headquarters is behind schedule. Your teams have not been on site for over two weeks, which has required us to push the entire project back. We just don't have flexibility on the timeline for this project, because the building must be ready for occupancy on July 1. Imbroglio's current lease expires then, and they have no other options.

Xavier, I've left three voice mails for you in the past week, but haven't heard back. Time is running out. Please call me so we can get a realistic plan in place to put this project back on track. That way we'll both feel proud of the work we have done on this one, too, and can look forward to many more successful collaborations in the future.

Sincerely,

Terry McGraw

Communicating with Customers: Loyalty

Sometimes the best way to motivate customers to remain loyal is to let them know you appreciate their business. That's how Joe Girard became the most successful salesperson in history (at least according to the *Guinness Book of World Records*). Once a month he sent every customer, prospect, and lead a greeting card (this was back before the days of e-mail) with the same message inside: *I like you!* Joe was selling Chevrolets in Detroit, so he had to do something to build customer loyalty. His product wasn't unique and price was moot, since most of his customers got the employee discount from General Motors. All he could think to do was remind everyone he appreciated them. But it worked. In fact, he sold more cars by himself from a table in the corner of the showroom than 95 percent of all the dealerships in North America!

Other than at the end of a transaction, people just don't hear "thank you" very often. They definitely don't hear "I like you" in a business setting. Usually, any message they get from a vendor has an ulterior, self-serving purpose shining through it. If you want to build customer loyalty, communicate personally with each customer four to six times a year. The more personal your message sounds, the better. Try to deliver a message that will be of interest to each customer but that doesn't come across as self-serving. Here's an example:

Subject: Housing options for Becky near Wrigleyville

Hi, Jane—

I remember you saying your daughter is moving to Chicago and wants to live in the city. The attached link tells about some cool, new spaces that are being developed near Wrigley Field. Apparently that's a very "in" area, the perfect spot for a young professional like Becky.

Just wanted to pass this on in case it's helpful to her. Gotta look out for my favorite clients and their kids, you know!

Regards,

Tim

Communicating with Investors: Commitment

When a business accepts investment funds, that business has a fiduciary responsibility to communicate clearly and accurately how the business is doing. Investors want to see the numbers, want to understand whether their investment is growing, and want to understand whether key performance measures have been achieved. They also want to know what the company's plans are, where opportunities lie, which threats to growth management is concerned about, and so on. Obviously, publicly traded companies use standard documents, including the annual report, the 10Q and 10K reports, press releases, analyst briefings, and many other types of messages to communicate with investors and the investment community. If you are with a small company or if you are privately held and have received a loan or sold a piece of the company to a silent partner, you need to communicate just like the big guys do. Besides the typical documents, such as an annual report or quarterly financial statements, look for opportunities to keep your investors informed about both positive and negative developments.

Subject: Recent hiring activity at Celludex

Jim, Ralph, and Barney—

At the last board meeting we identified three critical hires for Celludex. The first was a CFO with experience in mergers and acquisitions to support our growth strategy for next year. The second was a top-flight national account manager for the Southeast region, especially someone who is experienced in negotiating with major players in our market. The third was an experienced customer support manager who could introduce more consistency in our customer operation and who is knowledgeable in all three areas.

I'm writing to let you know that we have been successful in the first two goals and have three strong candidates for the customer support position.

We have made an offer to Bertha Gustafson to become our CFO. She served as CFO for Pillter during their recent M&A activity, which

continued

culminated in a highly successful public offering. We feel very fortunate to have a person of her experience joining the team.

We have already hired Bob Allen Wingate (yes, he likes to be called Bob Allen), who is based in Atlanta. Bob Allen has an outstanding record in sales and was the number one or two sales rep for the past six years for our top competitor, YTY. They had no noncompetes in place and in their recent reorganization wiped out half of Bob Allen's territory, so he was eager to make a move. With his existing client relationships and industry knowledge, we're confident he'll have an immediate impact on revenue generation.

We will interview our three candidates next week. One came from a recommendation from a current employee in our customer service organization, who recommended her former boss. The other two were referred to us by an executive recruiting firm we hired. On paper all three look well-qualified, so the interviews and reference checking will be critical.

There has been other good news this quarter, but nothing that can't wait for the board meeting on the 27th. See you then!

Regards,

Blaine

Communicating Bad News

Business is an arena of human endeavor, which means things don't go perfectly. People make mistakes. Markets fail to grow. Products arrive late, projects run over budget, jobs are outsourced, a major account cancels its contract, the firm's CEO ends up doing the perp walk on the evening news. Bad news can take lots of forms, and all of us will be forced to communicate it at various points in our careers. The question is, how should we do it?

One of the best pieces of management advice I ever received was that "bad news doesn't get better with age." Communicating bad news as soon as you have all the facts and can provide accurate information is better than delaying the message. But that feels risky. If we're communicating bad news up the chain of command, we may worry about our vulnerability. After all, some managers blame the messenger, and most of us don't want to be blamed. Some of us are like Michael Scott in *The Office:* We'd rather be liked than effective. We want to be seen as the good guy, the hero, so delivering bad news is extremely difficult for us. And some of us know that bad news can destroy strong motivation and high morale among employees, so we resist sharing it. In all of these situations, we need to communicate bad news in a way that minimizes the negative consequences, for ourselves and for others, and that sets the foundation for a more positive view of what's happening.

First, if at all possible, avoid communicating seriously bad news (such as termination, salary reduction, or layoffs) via e-mail or any other medium other than face-to-face discussion. The impersonality of a letter, an e-mail, a video broadcast, or a one-way conference call can make the employee feel disrespected. However, even if you are able to deliver the bad news in person, you still need to document it in writing, so it's worth thinking about how to do that successfully.

My second piece of advice is going to sound like something your Aunt Bea might say, but the only way to deliver bad news and have any hope of rebuilding morale, motivation, and trust is to communicate it as honestly and accurately as you can. Honesty really is the best policy. And if your company hasn't been delivering honest and direct communications on a consistent basis, don't expect to remake the culture into one of trust and openness overnight. That's not going to happen.

Avoid the temptation to lapse into Guff or Weasel. Managers use that kind of language to avoid saying something unpleasant in a direct manner. But people see through it immediately. If anything, you'll make your audience more anxious if you use Guff or Weasel, because they'll be worried that not only is the company's situation bad, but the leadership apparently isn't up to the task of dealing with it.

Likewise, avoid the temptation to lie, deny, minimize, or spin. You may gain a brief respite from an uncomfortable situation by doing those things, but eventually those tactics make bad situations worse. The strongest communication channel in any business is the grapevine. If you don't step forward to provide accurate information, the grapevine will start humming, filling the void with rumors, fears, and innuendos. People want to know what's going on, and they'll seek any source for the information they want.

The following is an e-mail following up from a face-to-face session with an employee. It starts with positive comments, because the employee has made a number of positive contributions, which are worthy of notice. It then clearly states the bad news: The employee must change his patterns of behavior, particularly when interacting with other employees, or face serious consequences. Finally, it lays out a "get well" plan for this employee, specifying what the employee must do to meet management's expectations:

Subject: Summary of today's review of your performance

Noah,

This morning in my office, you, Jan Powers of Human Resources, and I discussed your recent job performance and the steps you must take to bring it to a satisfactory level.

There is no question that you have made some useful contributions to the company as a technical support technician. You have been willing to come in early and stay late to help in a crisis situation. For example, you began setting up the new product training class when you saw nothing had been set up. You also found a cheaper way to support our web server and acted on it. You have in-depth knowledge of most technology and have provided support to the development team in resolving server problems.

However, your communication style has created problems for other members of the team and for your internal customers. For example, when the development team was considering a new feature for Release 4.0, you sent the entire team an e-mail titled "Another Bad Idea." In another instance, when Shawna Hensley asked you for help in doing a broadcast voicemail, you did not return her phone call for three days.

Another problem arises from the fact that if you do not consider a problem to be critical, you ignore it. This creates problems for other members of the team. For example, when Clark Castner needed a partition on his new computer, he could not get you to commit to a date that you would set it up. It was very frustrating for him and for Clark's manager, because without the partition Clark was not able to do his work. Also, you did not meet your target date for preparing the Release 4.0 test plan.

The most serious issue, however, is the fact that you have not accomplished the key goals you agreed to at your six-month review and have acted without authorization to install software on the corporate system:

1. At your six-month review, you agreed to meet weekly with your supervisor to review accomplishments and set priorities for the coming week. You have not met with her once in the six-month period.
2. In addition, you committed to establishing a system back-up process and running it daily. However, back-ups are not regularly performed. Eugene Farling has asked for three weeks for a back-up to development work that crashed, but to date you have not provided one.
3. Finally, you installed a program to monitor e-mails without authorization. You indicated this morning that you did this to track server volume, but the program also enables you to read all of the e-mails written by and to every employee in the company. This is a violation of trust that should not have happened and an action that exceeds your authority or scope of responsibilities.

Noah, you have good technical skills but without better communication skills, improved time management, and better follow-through you will not reach your potential in the company and will not perform at a satisfactory level. Together at today's meeting we agreed to a six-month probationary period during which you will accomplish three goals:

1. You will work with Ethan Dunn and Kirk Laine to deinstall the e-mail monitoring software immediately.
2. You will work with an outside coach who will help you develop the communication skills and time management ability you need to succeed in your role and move forward in your career. The company will help you select a coach and must approve your choice. At a minimum you must meet with the coach twelve

continued

times during the next six months at regular intervals. This coaching process must begin no later than two weeks from today.

3. You must meet weekly with your manager to review work completed and to set priorities for the coming week. There will be no exceptions to this requirement.

Failure to meet these three goals will require that the company take strong disciplinary measures. Noah, we are confident that you have much to offer the company and that the company can provide you with a satisfying and rewarding position. We look forward to seeing you accomplish these goals so you can move forward with us.

Brinsley Schwartz, Director of Operations
Jan Powers, Senior Consultant, Human Resources

Writing to Persuade

Persuasive writing often involves sales-related communications. You want to convince a prospect to agree to a meeting. You want to recommend that a current customer renew its contract or upgrade to something new. You want to close a piece of business by writing an effective proposal.

Persuasion can also involve convincing internal audiences to take an action you believe is right, to spend money on something you think is important, or to authorize a program you want to see implemented. Oddly enough, internal audiences are often more difficult to persuade than those outside the company. Perhaps they know us too well? Perhaps they don't give our recommendations the same focused attention they give to those coming from outside? Or perhaps we don't try as hard to communicate persuasively because we assume the needs and the potential outcomes are already obvious.

In both kinds of persuasion, using the right structural pattern is vital to success. Our goal is to deliver the right information in an order that corresponds to the way our reader's brain wants to receive it when he or she is making a decision.

As I said earlier in this book, persuasion is the most difficult form of writing for the vast majority of professionals. For people who are by nature technical and analytical in their thinking, persuasion often seems like an impenetrable mystery. They believe that facts presented logically should be enough to convince someone else. For people who work in sales but think their success is based on being charismatic and engaging, the concept of persuasive structure may seem irrelevant. It's all about relationships, right? Well, no, it's not only about relationships and it's not strictly about logic, either. You do need to have enough of a relationship with your decision maker that you have insight into what he or she thinks has highest priority in terms of needs or problems and potential impact. And you do need to be logical in the sense that you are using persuasive structure, the NOSE (Needs—Outcomes—Solution—Evidence) pattern. Putting those elements together will produce the right results.

Cold Call Messages—Introducing Yourself and Your Company

Writing a "cold call" message is tough. You're probably writing to a top executive, someone whose attention span is measured in nanoseconds and whose workload is crushing. In addition, if you're sending your cold call message via e-mail, you might be seen as just another irritating spammer. That means your first job is to avoid the "delete" button. You'll literally have no more than the first couple of lines to establish credibility and enough trust that your recipient keeps reading. It's not easy, but here are some guidelines that will help.

Prepare   Forget about sending the same message to everybody. If you're sending out a dozen or a hundred or a million messages, all of them saying the same thing, then I'm sorry to be the one to tell you this, but you are a spammer. A personal message is the only way you've got a chance at establishing rapport, credibility, and trust. Focus on rapport first, which, in a business setting, is primarily based on your ability to demonstrate knowledge and insight relevant to the audience. Preparation is the answer. A study done by the University of North Carolina's business school found that when top-level executives were asked what it would take for them to listen to a sales message, the most frequent answer was, "Show that you understand my business." The principle of first impressions is important here. You have to establish immediately that you know what you're talking about.

Do a little research. Check out the company's Web site. Look for recent news articles. Google the name of the executive to whom you are writing. Your goal is to get enough data, enough insight, to demonstrate that you know something about the company's business, that you can speak to its issues. That's the bait you put on the hook. Show that you are aware of the kind of business it's in, the goals, objectives, key initiatives, and recent announcements. There are three Cs that almost all top-level executives care about: customers, competitors, and comparables. Can you help the business improve relationships with customers? Can you give it insight or a competitive advantage over competitors? And do you have comparable experience that is likely to be successful in this executive's environment?

You need to do this quickly, so the subject line is a great place to put something specific to your recipient. How many times have you deleted an e-mail because you didn't recognize the sender and the subject looked generic?

Claim Your Right   Establish your "right" to write. Sending an e-mail to someone just because you want to is not enough of a reason. You need something more compelling than that. The best justification you can claim is that you were referred to this person by someone in his or her own organization. Oddly enough, this reason for writing often carries more weight than the fact that the reader him- or herself invited you to. At trade shows, conferences, or other networking events, people exchange cards and say, "Send me an e-mail; that sounds interesting," without really meaning it. By the time you write, they may have forgotten what you were talking about. But if you write because their colleague, subordinate, or friend recommended it, their interest is piqued. Both approaches work better than your third option, which is that you have recognized a compelling opportunity to help them and their organizations. Their reaction is likely to be skepticism. It'll be a tough sell at best. One way to overcome their skepticism is to mention someone else in their industry for whom you have achieved results. And that leads us to the next step:

Show Them the Money!   Quickly focus on value or impact and back it up with proof. What kind of impact is most likely to be an attention grabber for this prospect? Given your research, what kind of results are most likely to make your reader pause and read more carefully?

Avoid the Self-Centered Trap   The one thing you cannot under any circumstances do, if you hope to get your message through, is to start by talking about yourself or your company. That's deadly. It's of absolutely no interest to the prospect. If your message starts that way, the reader will hit "delete" before she's finished the first sentence.

Here's an example of a cold call message that isn't going to work:

Subject: Introducing myself

Dear Mr. Rowe,

I am writing to introduce myself to you as your new national account manager for Introversion Packaging Systems. We provide a full range of packaging solutions, including paper, Tyvek, plastic, and cardboard containers for products that range from granular or powder formulations through fragile manufactured products, including electronics. We can handle the requirements associated with food, pharmaceuticals, time-sensitive materials and other specialty applications. And we have worked with most of the major providers of packaging equipment so we can introduce our solutions without disrupting your current processing line.

If you have any questions or would like to discuss your packaging needs, please just respond to this e-mail or call me at the number below.

Sincerely,

Tovah Kahane
National Account Manager
Introversion Packaging Systems
555-456-7890

Why would Mr. Rowe read beyond the first sentence? In fact, why would he read beyond the subject line. "Introducing myself"? Oh, please. But suppose Tovah had done some research, had found a referral, and put together a message like the following. Don't you think the chances of making contact would be higher?

Subject: The linear microchip line—solving the packaging problems

Dear Mr. Rowe,

Sally Fink in your product development team suggested I contact you about the challenges you are facing in packaging your innovative line of linear microchips.

From what Sally said and from reading the last 10K report, I understand that the linear microchip is a potential blockbuster product for Sukhatta Micro Technologies. However, you are facing a tough challenge in figuring out how to package and ship the processors in a way that minimizes damage. The long, thin design, which is integral to increasing processing speeds to unparalleled levels, also makes the chips difficult to handle. They are more prone to breakage than traditional rectangular shapes.

Based on the projections in Sukhatta's 10K, reducing breakage from the current level of 2.5 percent to an acceptable six sigma level of performance would mean an additional $42 million in sales. In addition, there would be reduced expenses from handling returns and improved customer satisfaction.

At Introversion Packaging Systems we specialize in handling exactly these kinds of challenges. For example, for a major pharmaceutical manufacturer, we developed an innovative system for shipping and delivering a very fragile medical device to hospitals and clinics where it is used. We were able to reduce losses from breakage from over 7 percent to less than one in a million. The solution for them involved using a Tyvek container filled with air at high enough pressure to hold the product in suspension.

That solution might work for Sukhatta or we may need to explore other options. In over twenty years of high-tech packaging experience, we have established a reputation as the leader in developing innovative approaches to our clients' needs. I am writing to introduce myself to you and to suggest we schedule a phone call or an in-person visit to discuss how we can help.

I will call your office on Wednesday to schedule time on your calendar. I look forward to exploring packaging solutions with you that will make Sukhatta's line of linear microchips even more successful.

Sincerely,

Tovah Kahane
National Account Manager
Introversion Packaging Systems
555-456-7890

Setting a Meeting

Let's suppose our message interests Ramsey Rowe, the executive we contacted about packaging Sukhatta's new linear microchips. Now we need to sell him on meeting with us. Even though he has expressed some interest in what we have to offer, we shouldn't assume that setting up the meeting isn't a persuasive writing task.

Subject: Agenda and timing for our meeting

Mr. Rowe—

Thanks for your quick response. It appears Sally was right about there being a good fit between your needs for innovative packaging and what we can provide. We've solved similar problems for Nielssen Technology and Azimuth Computer Systems. I'm confident you can profit from our experience, too.

I recommend a one-hour meeting to discuss: (1) the parameters of your linear microchips, (2) your manufacturing process, (3) the ship-

continued

ping options your customers require, (4) the packaging problems you are currently experiencing, and (5) the budget you have established for resolving these problems. By the way, we recognize you will be sharing highly sensitive, proprietary business information with us. We will be happy to execute a mutual nondisclosure agreement between our firms.

I will bring Todd Higbee and Anne Lukajs to the meeting. Between them they have more than twenty years' experience in designing high-tech packaging solutions.

Can we meet next Tuesday or Wednesday? I'd like to schedule our meeting soon, because Todd will be in Denmark for two weeks and I want to make sure we can take advantage of his expertise before he leaves. I'll call your office to set a date and time that work for you.

I'm confident that your investment of an hour or so in meeting with us will pay big dividends. We're excited to explore the situation and offer you our expertise.

Regards,

Tovah

Following Up from a Meeting

The meeting went very well. Ramsey was open and candid, and he had a production designer attend who was able to explain the product challenges in greater depth. They both seemed very interested in what you and your colleagues had to share. You asked the appropriate qualifying questions and feel confident there's a real opportunity here. So now what?

You need to follow up as quickly as possible after the meeting. Your goal is to validate what you have heard, to make sure you have it right, and to set the agenda for next steps. You are trying to maintain momentum and interest and move what is now a qualified opportunity further into the sales cycle. Here's the kind of message you want to send.

Subject: Following up from Tuesday's meeting; next steps

Ramsey—

Thanks again for meeting with me, Todd, and Anne. Your insights and the information that Derrick provided are extremely helpful in developing a packaging solution that will deliver bottom-line business results for Sukhatta.

You and Derrick indicated that your key areas of concern are:
- Reducing breakage during the shipping process.
- Providing a packaging system that's easy to open without risking damage to the microchips.
- Keeping total packaging costs under 15 cents per item.
- Labeling the packages to provide strong branding for the linear chips and for Sukhatta.

As promised, Todd, Anne, and I will review your needs in light of similar packaging problems we have handled. We know it's important to take into account all of the challenges you face, including unit costs and branding. We will focus on delivering a technically sound solution that also delivers the right business results. Based on our analysis, we will evaluate all the options and will develop high-level recommendations for you.

Once we have developed those recommendations, which will take approximately ten to fifteen days, the next steps in the process include:
- Review the recommendations with you, Derrick, and other members of the Sukhatta team
- Establish an agreement to proceed between our firms
- Interview your operations manager and conduct a site visit to the manufacturing facilities used to produce the linear microchip
- Interview your marketing team to confirm branding and labeling requirements
- Establish a prototype packaging system
- Conduct pilot tests on the prototype
- Review and amend the prototype for full production
- Move into full-scale implementation of the new packaging system

I look forward to discussing our initial recommendations with you, on or before September 15. If we can gain initial concurrence by then

continued

on the technical approach we recommend, we can meet your timeline of completing the project by the end of this calendar year.

Introversion is committed to working with you to build a mutually
successful business relationship and to deliver bottom-line results for
Sukhatta with your exciting new product line.

Regards,

Tovah

Announcing a New Product or Service

It's easier to sell to existing customers than to new ones, so when you
have a new product or service, you're likely to turn to your current
customer base first. Again, we can't afford to treat this as an instance
of writing to inform. Even though they know you and like you, they
may not be interested in your new stuff unless you persuasively show
them that it solves a problem, meets a need, and delivers a big payoff.

Resist the temptation to lapse into Geek speak. Even though existing customers have a higher level of tolerance for your in-house
jargon than a brand new prospect is likely to have, you will communicate more successfully if you keep your language as simple,
clear, and direct as possible. Demonstrate that you know them, understand their business, and are writing because you think this will
benefit them, not because its in your own interests to do so.

Ms. Sandra Jameson
Vice President of Sales
Nova Cellular, Inc.
88 Montgomery Road
Suite 1400
Cincinnati, Ohio 45212

Dear Ms. Jameson:

I know you want to stay informed about developments that relate
to your responsibilities, your business, and your industry. We

appreciate being part of your success for the past six years, so we're excited to share some important news with you.

Many of our clients have spoken with us about the problem of developing greater customer loyalty and return business. Customer churn has become one of the biggest challenges in the cellular marketplace. What we have developed is a solution specifically designed to help cellular service providers like Nova improve communication with customers, increase customer loyalty, and maintain sales momentum. Initial field tests indicate the positive impact in all three areas will be significant. In fact, our test markets showed a decline in customer defections of 34% and revenue growth of 17%.

What we have developed is similar to the affinity marketing approaches used by credit card providers to encourage use of their particular card. However, our approach goes beyond the traditional limits of these programs by allowing users to establish multiple affinity relationships and by delivering affinity-related content directly to their cellular device.

If you agree with me that this is something that could benefit Nova, I would enjoy talking with you about it at your convenience. Would Thursday morning work for you? I'll call to confirm the appointment or to schedule one more convenient for you.

It's exciting for us at Root Cause Marketing to be able to offer leading edge solutions to our clients, and it's also a great opportunity for Nova to gain competitive advantage. I look forward to talking with you soon.

Sincerely,

Tim Southerland
CEO

Responding to a Request for Information

If a customer or prospect calls or e-mails us and asks for some information, we might assume that our task is one where we must write to inform. That means we use the funnel pattern, giving the other person the bit of information they want first. But if this is a selling situation, we should write our message persuasively.

Keeping in mind the fundamental NOSE pattern, organize your response into four sections:

Greeting   Address the customer by name. Automated response systems seldom do this correctly, so they create instant cognitive dissonance. As a human being, you can do better. Also, link your opening paragraph to the writer's inquiry or to any specific conversations, e-mail exchanges, or other contact you may have had. This will establish relevance and context.

Use a conversational tone. Do not lapse into Guff. This is not the time to try to impress the reader. Avoid using the typical stuffy business clichés, like "Per our conversation . . . " or "Pursuant to your request . . . "

Current Situation (customer needs and issues)   This section itemizes the key business and technical concerns for this customer. Use bullet points and guard against using Geek in this section. Identify not only the situation that needs to be addressed, but also why it is a problem from a business perspective.

Your Unique Value   This section addresses your company's differentiators and why they add value. Your goal in this section is to establish your firm as a preferred provider. Avoid lapsing in to Fluff—*best of breed, uniquely qualified, state of the art.* Be specific and focus the customer on value instead of price.

Closing   End with a polite close that is also a call to action. Do not use the typical cliché closing, "If you have any questions, please feel free to call." Keep control of the buying situation by indicating when and how you will follow up, if appropriate.

Greeting   · Dear James,

Thank you for your interest in CallCentric. You inquired in your e-mail about our ability to provide inbound call center support in a technical environment. We are confident we can offer Electomek the finest in call center operations.

Current situation

In fact, CallCentric has helped high-tech companies from all over North America handle their call center requirements. Some typical challenges we have helped our customers address include:

- One customer needed to reduce the cost of call center support without reducing quality. Call-Centric was able to take over the call center operation, lowering total costs by 35%.
- Another CallCentric customer was introducing a complex new product and needed a highly educated call center staff. We met the challenge by drawing from one of the most highly educated work forces in North America.

Value proposition

CallCentric offers unique value to our customers. We can set up, staff, and operate a call center, typically at a fraction of the cost that the same center can be set up in other areas. And because we are based in North America, our agents represent your company in the most professional manner possible.

Closing

James, I will call you shortly to discuss your needs, desired outcomes, and your decision process. Based on that discussion, I can prepare a detailed proposal for you.

CallCentric looks forward to helping you implement an effective solution to improve call center operations at Electomek so that your business can continue to grow.

Regards,

Ari Kirkaijian
National Account Manager
CallCentric Inc.

Checking on Customer Satisfaction

Seeking feedback from customers on how well they like the services or products you provide can be frustrating. How many "surveys" from hotels, rental car companies, and other firms have you received, either electronically or on paper, only to ignore them? Most of us don't want to bother unless we feel a strong need to complain. To break through and get a response, keep the survey short and simple. Making your request personal will also help. Here's an example of a letter that might pull a higher response:

Ms. Kalyn Bugg
Vice President of Operations
Buckeye Feed and Supply
7623 Reed Hartmann Highway
Cincinnati, Ohio 45212

Dear Ms. Bugg:

Thank you for the cooperation you and your entire team at Buckeye Feed and Supply provided us throughout all phases of project to update your accounting systems. We will consider our work complete with your approval.

We are very concerned about your satisfaction and the satisfaction of all of our customers. As a result, I am writing to ask you a favor. Are you available on Friday, April 20, for a half-hour phone call to discuss:

1. What exceeded your expectations?
2. What fell short of your expectations?
3. What results are you seeing so far from your accounting system?
4. What you would do differently next time?

We will use your comments to modify our methods and processes, if necessary, so that we deliver outstanding results and a superior experience for our customers.

Sincerely,

Kent Arsgrove
Project Manager

Nurture Messages

A nurture message is not aimed at selling a particular product or service. Instead, it's intended, as the name implies, to nurture a relationship between you and the customer. Earlier I mentioned the father of nurture messages, Joe Girard, and how his practice of sending out a greeting card once a month to everyone in his mailing list directly led to a fabulously successful career selling cars. Even if you're selling complex services or highly abstract intellectual capital—in fact, I'd say *especially* if that's your situation—a consistent program of sending nurture messages to your clients, prospects, and others in the community of interest will help you succeed, too.

For example, suppose you're an attorney specializing in probate issues with a practice aimed at helping families establish self-directed trusts to preserve their assets. Why would a client come to you instead of a different attorney? Maybe because you were recommended? Maybe because she met you through some kind of community service work or social activity? Or maybe because you have regularly provided useful information that people appreciate? Jim Cecil, the guru of nurture marketing, has found that sending out two or three messages doesn't have much impact on business. But by the time you have sent out eight or nine, good things start to happen. Customers and prospects will have a "top-of-mind" awareness of you and your business after getting that many messages from you, so if they need the kinds of products or services you provide, they think of you first. Sales will start to soar.

The idea of a nurture message is to build rapport and establish your value as a knowledgeable expert. Nurture messages are not intended to make a specific sales pitch. If you're trying to build business at your auto repair shop and you send out a monthly coupon offering ten dollars off an oil change, that may build traffic but it's not a nurture message. Here's an example of a nurture message that the owner of an auto repair shop might send as one among a series of monthly messages:

Subject: Are synthetic oils worth the extra money?

Synthetic motor oils cost more than traditional motor oils. But are they worth it?

Recent research from an independent testing laboratory confirmed that using synthetic oils in your car is worth the extra money. The lab found that at very low temperatures (start up) and at high temperatures (extended high-speed driving) the synthetic oils provided much greater performance in terms of protecting engine parts against wear. In addition, the research found that synthetic oils tend to evaporate less than traditional petroleum-based oils, and they have greater resistance to clogging or the formation of sludge and deposits.

From a practical standpoint, the fact that synthetic oils last longer means that their main disadvantage—they cost more—is less of an issue than it appears. In addition, because you can change your oil less often if you use a synthetic, they have less of an environmental impact.

In short, for today's cars the best choice is a synthetic oil, especially if you plan to drive your more than 100,000 miles. At Albert's Auto Works, we carry a full line of both traditional and synthetics and will be happy to explain which particular oil is right for your vehicle.

Happy driving!

Recommendations and Proposals

I wrote a whole book, *Persuasive Business Proposals,* on the subject of writing persuasive sales proposals. It's a complex subject, particularly when you take into account the difficulties involved in responding to a difficult request for proposal, the challenges of coordinating a whole team of contributors, and the pressures of working under extremely tight deadlines. The core of that message, though, is the same one I have been preaching here. If you want to write to persuade, use the right structural pattern.

Here's an example of an executive summary written to convince a firm that's in some financial trouble that it would be wise to outsource basic maintenance operations. The executive summary starts by defining a problem that matters to the customer, a regional chain of newspapers. It then shows that there's a potentially big payoff from solving this problem. Next, it proposes a solution. Finally, it provides evidence that the vendor submitting this proposal is qualified to handle the job.

Executive Summary

The recent acquisition of The American Newspaper Federation by Kipper and Townsend Financial Partners confirms the fact that there is tremendous value in your assets and operations. You have an outstanding portfolio, with the leading regional newspapers, the leading free alternative papers, and the leading shoppers' tabloid. You have recently launched a Web site, which provides regional news and expanded coverage as a supplement to your print publications. However, your acquisition by Kipper and Townsend has increased pressure on ANF's management to increase profits and generate a significant return for your investors.

You indicated during our meetings that you need to decrease total employment by approximately 150 full-time equivalent employees—around 13% of your total workforce. Your goal in making those reductions, however, is to preserve your core competency and your journalistic strengths. To do that you must focus on eliminating jobs that are peripheral to your revenue-generating activities. This is important because weakening the actual product is not an option. You face tough competition from a variety of other newspapers, from TV and radio journalism, and from nontraditional sources of information such as Yahoo and Google.

As you have recognized, the people who service and maintain your facilities throughout the region contribute to your success by providing a decent working environment, but they are not a part of your core business. They help provide the part of the business operation that creates the infrastructure within which your core activities function. In fact, cleaning and maintenance is so far removed from your core business in some areas that these employees and their activities are not well documented or monitored.

continued

Outsourcing these services can deliver a rapid payback. Our proposal documents the potential savings for The American Newspaper Federation and shows that you can reduce fixed costs by approximately $150,000 a year. A second important outcome from outsourcing is that you will reduce your full-time headcount by the 20 to 25 employees who currently provide cleaning and maintenance services. This takes a big bite out of the total goal of a 150-person reduction.

We recommend that you hire us to provide all of your cleaning and maintenance services in all of your locations. We will implement documented systems and tools and provide bonded personnel who are trained to do this work in the most efficient way. We will look for opportunities to consolidate services to save you more money and will recommend steps to streamline the services where possible. For example, for some of your small offices, we may be able to clean the office with the same crew that cleans another client's facilities nearby. That results in substantial cost savings for you. In the body of our proposal we have outlined our three-step process for transitioning your current maintenance staff to our employment.

There are two important reasons that we are confident we will be successful in providing you with these services.
1. We have recently completed exactly this kind of project for the Wide Channel family of radio stations. Although their offices are different from yours, their needs and concerns were the same. We have included a case study and reference from Wide Channel that documents the outstanding results we delivered.
2. Because of our size and our national presence, we can quickly adapt to any sudden changes in your operations. We can scale up or down, if you go through further merger and acquisition activity. We can also provide additional services, such as security or catering, if you decide to pursue further outsourcing opportunities.

We fully understand that this is a challenging time for the newspaper industry as a whole. The American Newspaper Federation has received a valuable infusion of capital, but you need effective partners who can help you deliver significant bottom line returns. We are eager to work with you to help you achieve your goals by implementing the recommendations we have made.

Presenting a New Idea to Management or Colleagues

The internal audience can be as tough a customer as you're likely to find. You have to convince management to spend precious resources or to reallocate priorities in ways they weren't anticipating.

Subject: The need to increase participation in the Honors Program

Dear President Bollmer and Chancellor Wing:

Our Honors Program at Missouri Institute of Technology has experienced declining enrollment over the past four years. In raw numbers, Honors enrollment has gone from a high of 256 four years ago to 181 this year, even though total enrollment has increased by 400 students.

The problem: This is a problem for the school because the Honors Program is a showcase of our best students and provides an opportunity for our leading instructors to develop innovative curriculum. If enrollment dwindles further, both students and faculty will lose interest and Missouri IT will lose prestige among other colleges.

The impact: On the other hand, if we can increase participation in the Honors Program, the college as a whole gains. Besides the prestige factor, increased enrollment in Honors means that more students will be doing Honors projects. These involve a combination of research and service to the college that often has significant value. For our faculty, having more Honors students will mean more opportunity to conduct Honors classes. In the past, these have been the source of some of our most creative teaching and the Honors courses faculty members have designed have led directly to at least three books and several articles. Finally, graduating larger number of Honors students will be good for placement. Employers and graduate schools look favorably on Honors graduates and on schools with strong Honors programs.

Our recommendations: We recommend making participation in the Honors Program more attractive for students. There are four inexpensive steps we can take immediately.

First, let's allow members of the Honors Program to enroll in their classes before the general student body. Being able to get any classes

continued

---

they want will have real value for students, yet costs the college almost nothing.

Second, let's offer our Honors Program students special parking privileges. Besides putting them at the head of the line during the parking lottery, there are some other things we could do with this coveted privilege. One option would be to give them a reduced rate on parking; another would be to give them the option of getting an assignment in any lot of their choice.

Third, let's give our Honors students the same library privileges that graduate students have.

Fourth, let's highlight our Honors students by having them go first at graduation ceremonies. We can list them on the first few pages of the program, have them come forward for their diplomas first, and make sure everyone understands that the only way to graduate *summa cum laude* or *magna cum laude* is by participating in the Honors Program at Missouri Institute of Technology.

Fifth, let's have the Office of Public Affairs issue press releases on each of the Honors projects, both to the local media and to newspapers in the students' hometowns.

Looking at the longer term and recognizing that our final recommendation may require some funding to execute, we also recommend setting aside a special dorm as the Honors Dorm or Honors House. This will give our Honors students the opportunity to live in the same space and get better acquainted with each other.

Next steps: With your authorization, we propose to invite participation from current members of the Honors Program, both students and faculty, to brainstorm additional ideas for attracting increased enrollment and to implement the five ideas we have outlined above. We believe that coverage of these innovations in the campus newspaper will provide the Program with positive publicity. That alone may have a positive impact on enrollments.

Great schools have great students. We have some wonderful students who are committed to graduating in the Honors Program. But we believe we have many others who are capable of participating and of discovering their own academic excellence. Our recommendations will reach those students, enriching their college experience and enhancing Missouri Institute of Technology as well.

May we proceed to form a committee of students and faculty to implement the five ideas we have outlined, to brainstorm new ideas, and to work to strengthen our Honors Program?

Sincerely,

Dr. William Roberts, Metallurgical Engineering
Dr. Victoria Barkhoff, Department of Psychology

CHAPTER 5

Your Potential

We've covered a lot of ground in this book. We've glanced at linguistic theory, and we've studied some practical applications. Out of all that material, what are the most important things to remember? What are the essential steps to make sure you write in the language of success? You're entitled to decide that for yourself, but here are five points that I think are critical:

1. **Tell the truth.** Life is too short to do anything else. And telling the truth makes it a lot easier to write clearly and concisely.
2. **Say it in your own voice.** To the extent possible, allowing for the differences between spoken and written language, write it the way you would say it.
3. **Reject the languages of Fluff, Guff, Geek, and Weasel.** They don't communicate. They don't impress other people. They don't work.
4. **Remember the "first time right" rule.** If your readers can understand what you wrote as soon as they read it, you wrote it well. If your readers have to go back and reread what you wrote, you didn't.
5. **Know why you're writing before you start so you can use the right pattern.** Whether you're writing to inform, to evaluate, or to persuade, using the right structural pattern will increase your effectiveness.

Writing is a skill. Like other skills we may have—cooking, riding a bicycle, playing the piano—our ability will improve if we practice a lot and if we acquire more knowledge. Some people also have unique talents, which is why we have the Julia Childs, Lance Armstrongs, and Oscar Petersons of our world. Don't tell yourself that you can't write because you don't have the talent for it. If you can talk, you can write. The more you practice and the more you learn, the better you'll be at it.

You have the potential to become fluent in the language of success. Good luck in achieving your potential.

Index

About the Author

Tom Sant, Ph.D., has had an extraordinary impact on the way professionals communicate. He is internationally recognized as a pioneer in bringing research and analytical methods to the field of business communication. His bestseller, *Persuasive Business Proposals,* transformed the way businesses write proposals and increased win ratios for hundreds of companies all over the world. His study of the fundamentals of professional sales, *The Giants of Sales,* traces the evolution of modern sales techniques, showing which techniques work and why, linking them to research and concepts in human psychology. Now, in *The Language of Success,* he has clearly identified the pseudo-languages—Fluff, Guff, Geek, and Weasel—that prevent people from communicating effectively and shows what it takes to write successfully.

Tom received his doctorate in English from UCLA. While teaching at the University of Cincinnati, he was invited by General Electric's Aircraft Engine Business Group to teach engineers how to write more clearly and concisely. The course was a smash hit, and he was soon asked by senior managers to help write high-value technical summaries, marketing materials, speeches, presentations, film scripts, and proposals. His success as a proposal writer was so outstanding that GE's top management asked him to train all of the Aircraft Engine Business Group's professional staff in using the techniques he had developed. At that point, Tom said goodbye to a career in academics and began consulting full time.

In the years since, Tom's innovative approach to proposal writing has had a profound impact on the way companies present their messages to prospects in all industries. For the first time, based on Tom's work, persuasion was seen as a process rather than a mystery, and writers were able to manage complex writing challenges with clear ideas of how to proceed. Proposals Tom has written directly for clients have now won over $30 billion in contracts, but by applying his concepts, professionals have won many times that amount on their own. In recognition of his lifetime contributions to the profession of proposal writing, Tom was named the first-ever Fellow of the Association of Proposal Management Professionals in 2001.

Since his early success with General Electric, many other companies have hired Tom to help them handle their communication challenges, including Procter & Gamble, AT&T, Microsoft, Johnson Controls, Booz Allen, NCR, Accenture, Dell, HSBC, Motorola, Kaiser Permanente, and hundreds more. His writing has received numerous awards, including the Gold Medal at the New York Industrial Film Festival for best script, the IABC Gold Quill for best video script, the Silver Telly for best nonbroadcast video and film script, and the Platinum Award from the MarCom association for outstanding writing in an electronic newsletter, an award won in competition against more than 3,000 other entries.

As a speaker and trainer, Tom has helped thousands of professionals improve their ability to deliver the right message the right way. *Selling Power Magazine* named him one of the top ten sales trainers in the world, and he has been a popular keynote speaker at conferences around the world, from New York and London to Istanbul and Perth.

Tom's interest in the use of technology to facilitate communications led him to invent the world's first proposal automation system in 1991, the first Web-based content configuration system for producing proposals, letters, and presentations in 1995, and the first system for automatically analyzing and responding to complex RFPs. These systems are used by thousands of companies around the world.

Tom lives with his wife, Susan Hirsch, in San Luis Obispo, California.